BAPTISTWAYPRESS®

Adult Bible Study Guide

The Letter to the Romans

What God Is Up To

Wesley Shotwell

Ebbie Smith

Kathy Robinson Hillman

BAPTISTWAYPRESS®

Dallas, Texas

BAPTISTWAY PRESS® Management Team
Executive Director, Baptist General Convention of Texas: Charles Wade
Director, Missions, Evangelism, and Ministry Team: Wayne Shuffield
Ministry Team Leader: Phil Miller
Publisher, BAPTISTWAY PRESS®: Ross West

Cover and Interior Design and Production: Desktop Miracles, Inc.
Printing: Data Reproductions Corporation
Cover Photo: The Colosseum in Rome, istockphoto.com

First edition: September 2007
ISBN: 1–931060–93–2

How to Make the Best Use of This Issue

Whether you're the teacher or a student—

1. Start early in the week before your class meets.
2. Overview the study. Review the table of contents and read the study introduction. Try to see how each lesson relates to the overall study.
3. Use your Bible to read and consider prayerfully the Scripture passages for the lesson. (You'll see that each writer has chosen a favorite translation for the lessons in this issue. You're free to use the Bible translation you prefer and compare it with the translation chosen for that unit, of course.)
4. After reading all the Scripture passages in your Bible, then read the writer's comments. The comments are intended to be an aid to your study of the Bible.
5. Read the small articles—"sidebars"—in each lesson. They are intended to provide additional, enrichment information and inspiration and to encourage thought and application.
6. Try to answer for yourself the questions included in each lesson. They're intended to encourage further thought and application, and they can also be used in the class session itself.

If you're the teacher—

A. Do all of the things just mentioned, of course. As you begin the study with your class, be sure to find a way to help your class know the date on which each lesson will be studied. You might do this in one or more of the following ways:

  • In the first session of the study, briefly overview the study by identifying with your class the date on which each lesson will be studied. Lead your class to write the date in the table of contents on page 7 and on the first page of each lesson.
  • Make and post a chart that indicates the date on which each lesson will be studied.
  • If all of your class has e-mail, send them an e-mail with the dates the lessons will be studied.

3

- Provide a bookmark with the lesson dates. You may want to include information about your church and then use the bookmark as an outreach tool, too.
- Develop a sticker with the lesson dates, and place it on the table of contents or on the back cover.

B. Get a copy of the *Teaching Guide*, a companion piece to this *Study Guide*. The *Teaching Guide* contains additional Bible comments plus two teaching plans. The teaching plans in the *Teaching Guide* are intended to provide practical, easy-to-use teaching suggestions that will work in your class.

C. After you've studied the Bible passage, the lesson comments, and other material, use the teaching suggestions in the *Teaching Guide* to help you develop your plan for leading your class in studying each lesson.

D. You may want to get the additional adult Bible study comments— *Adult Online Bible Commentary*—by Dr. Jim Denison, pastor of Park Cities Baptist Church, Dallas, Texas, that are available at www.baptistwaypress.org and can be downloaded free. An additional teaching plan plus teaching resource items are also available at www.baptistwaypress.org.

E. You also may want to get the enrichment teaching help that is provided on the internet by the *Baptist Standard* at www.baptiststandard.com. (Other class participants may find this information helpful, too.) Call 214–630–4571 to begin your subscription to the printed edition of the *Baptist Standard*.

F. Enjoy leading your class in discovering the meaning of the Scripture passages and in applying these passages to their lives.

Writers of This Study Guide

Wesley Shotwell, writer of unit 1, lessons 1–5, is pastor of Ash Creek Baptist Church, Azle, Texas. Dr. Shotwell formerly was pastor of churches in Tennessee. He is a graduate of Baylor University (B.A.), Southwestern Baptist Theological Seminary (M.Div.), and Vanderbilt Divinity School (D.Min.).

Ebbie Smith wrote units 2 and 3, lessons 6–10. He is retired as professor of Christian Ethics and Missions, Southwestern Baptist Theological Seminary. Dr. Smith also served fifteen years as a missionary in Indonesia.

Kathy Robinson Hillman, writer of unit 4, lessons 11–13, is on faculty at Baylor University, where she is associate professor and acquisitions librarian. She served as president of Texas Woman's Missionary Union, 2000–2004. She grew up in First Baptist Church, Eldorado, Texas, and has received degrees from Baylor and the University of North Texas. She and her husband John have three children and are members of Columbus Avenue Baptist Church, Waco.

The Letter to the Romans: What God Is Up To

Date of Study

U N I T   O N E

Providing the Way Out

U N I T   T W O

Offering the Best Possible Life

ROMANS: *What God Is Up To*

If Paul had written his Letter to the Romans directly to you, what would the letter be saying? This question points to what we want to ask of every biblical book, of course, and ultimately that's the question each study in this Bible study series seeks to answer. We want to find how the text speaks to us, what it means for us, and how we can apply it today.

There is a place for Bible study that simply wants to deal with what a Bible book meant "back then," of course. That's the place this study of Romans, as well as our other studies, begins. Indeed, it's where we *must* begin. We must begin our study with what the Bible passage meant to its first readers in their life situation. Otherwise we too readily will import our own ideas and call them God's. That's why in this study of Romans we will seek first to understand the message Paul meant for the Roman Christians sometime in the mid to late 50s, or maybe early 60s, of the first century A.D. We do that by trying to discover as best we can the life situation with which these Roman Christians were dealing.

The Roman Christians' Life Situation

What do we know about what life was like for these Christians in the capital city of the Roman Empire? We will deal with at least some of the answers to that question as we move through the study of these lessons. Help in understanding what life was like for them can be found in the instructions Paul gave them and the message he proclaimed to them. Listening to one end of the conversation with the Romans—Paul's—can give us clues about the situation in which the Romans lived. Watch for these clues as you move through this study.

One important matter of which to be aware is that likely the church was composed of Christians who had come out of a pagan, Gentile background as well as of Christians who had come out of a Jewish background. They most likely were all first-generation Christians, only one step removed, if that, from their respective Jewish and Gentile backgrounds. It would have been easy for them to revert to their previous cultures in matters large and small rather than to continue to learn of Christ. Their faith in Christ united them, but they were still struggling to work out the details. Some of the details were so huge that they threatened to drive a wedge between these Christians based on their respective Jewish and Gentile backgrounds.

The situation in Rome itself would have contributed to potential conflicts between Gentile and Jewish Christians. Official Rome was opposed to the Jews, forcing many if not most to leave the city in the late 40s.[1] The Emperor Nero reversed this order in 54 A.D., close to the time Paul wrote to the Roman Christians. Many Jews who had been expelled returned, but open arms did not await them. Given what we ourselves know about the prejudicial treatment of minorities, can we not readily see that the cultural situation in Rome easily could have influenced the attitudes of Gentile Christians toward their fellow Christians from a Jewish background? Breaking down prejudice is generally not easy, even among Christians.

At least a part of what Paul's Letter to the Romans sought to do was to challenge and guide these Christians from different backgrounds back together and to keep them focused on their unity in their faith in Christ. As a leading Bible interpreter has written of current study on Paul's Letter to the Romans, "A consensus seems to be building . . . that the main need in the Roman church . . . was that of resolving the disunity between Jews and Gentiles. If so, then the spiritual gift Paul wanted to impart was his gospel, which was to be the basis of unity for the Roman congregations."[2] Paul sought to do this by helping all of them to understand what God was up to then and what God had been up to in the past in his dealings with Israel. Paul's overarching goal was to help them understand more, and more extensively, what God had done and was doing in Christ.

Note that early in his Letter to the Roman Christians, Paul wrote this about the gospel: "I am not ashamed of the gospel, because it is the power of God for the salvation of everyone who believes: first for the Jew, then for the Gentile" (Romans 1:16).[3] We may have read those words so often that we have to work hard to picture how they might have sounded when a small group of Jewish and Gentile Christians gathered in a home in Rome and first heard them read. Heads might suddenly have popped up, and then people might have looked around at one another and finally down at their sandals. Maybe someone asked that the verse be read again.

Then they began to pay more attention and to learn. Let us do that ourselves as we study Romans.

Toward a Rewarding Study

But first let us get ourselves ready. In past dealings with this book, even if you've just dipped into Romans here and there—and probably especially if you've just dipped in here and there—you've likely found that at least parts of it aren't completely clear on the surface. To say the least! You may have found it even more difficult to see the thrust of the Letter to the Romans as a whole.

If this describes your experience with the Letter to the Romans, you are not alone. As one of the premier New Testament interpreters and theologians of our day has written, "Perhaps not surprisingly, it remains the case that anyone who claims to understand Romans fully is, almost by definition, mistaken."[4]

Still, we will strive to understand this letter as best we can. Even more, we will attempt in this study to personalize its message. The results in doing so promise to be exceedingly great. Romans, while written to a particular group of Christians in a particular place at a particular time, is still written to all Christians in all times and places. As a leading interpreter of Paul's Letter to the Romans has written, "Romans, then, is an occasional letter but with universal applicability—not either-or but both-and."[5] Christians through the centuries, beginning with the first recipients, have found Romans to be Paul's most thorough and carefully reasoned explanation of the Christian faith. Romans deals with the deep and challenging questions of what the death and resurrection of one man, Jesus of Nazareth, means; what it means to say that Jesus *saves*; and what God's act in Jesus the Messiah means for how we are to live.

Units of Study

The titles for the study units attempt to give guidance for understanding what the Letter to the Romans suggests about "What God Is Up To," the subtitle of the study. God is "Providing the Way Out" (unit one), "Offering the Best Possible Life" (unit two), "Continuing to Care for the Jewish People" (unit three), and "Calling for Faithful Living" (unit four).

Additional Resources for Studying Paul's Letter to the Romans: [6]

Paul J. Achtemeier. *Romans*. Interpretation: A Bible Commentary for Teaching and Preaching. Atlanta, Georgia: John Knox Press, 1985.

William Barclay. *The Letter to the Romans*. The Daily Study Bible. Philadelphia: The Westminster Press, 1975.

James D.G. Dunn. *Romans 1—8*. Word Biblical Commentary. Volume 38a. Dallas: Word Books, 1988.

Herschel H. Hobbs. *Romans*. Waco, Texas: Word Books, 1977.

Craig S. Keener. *IVP Bible Background Commentary: New Testament*. Downers Grove, Illinois: InterVarsity Press, 1993.

J. W. MacGorman. *Romans: Everyman's Gospel*. Nashville: Convention Press, 1976.

Douglas Moo. *The Epistle to the Romans*. The New International Commentary on the New Testament. Eerdmans: Grand Rapids, 1996.

Douglas J. Moo. "Romans." *Zondervan Illustrated Bible Backgrounds Commentary*. Grand Rapids: Zondervan, 2002.

Dale Moody. "Romans." *The Broadman Bible Commentary*. Volume 10. Nashville, Tennessee: Broadman Press, 1970.

Robert H. Mounce. *Romans*. The New American Commentary. Volume 27. Nashville, Tennessee: Broadman and Holman Publishers, 1995.

A. T. Robertson. *Word Pictures in the New Testament*. Volume 4. Nashville, Tennessee: Broadman Press, 1931.

John R.W. Stott. *The Message of Romans: God's Good News for the World*. The Bible Speaks Today. Downers Grove, Illinois: InterVarsity Press, 2001.

Charles H. Talbert. *Romans*. Smyth and Helwys Bible Commentary. Macon, Georgia: Smyth and Helwys, 2002.

Curtis Vaughn and Bruce Corley. *Romans: A Study Guide*. Grand Rapids: Zondervan, 1976.

N. T. Wright. "The Letter to the Romans." *The New Interpreter's Bible*. Volume X. Nashville, Tennessee: Abingdon Press, 2002.

Unit one, "Providing the Way Out," consists of five lessons on Romans 1—4. The first lesson, "Connecting the Dots," is on the introductory verses of Romans. This passage and this lesson set the stage for the rest of the study. The next two lessons—"No Excuses, No Exceptions" (Romans 1:18–32; 2:1–13) and "Just Not Good Enough" (Romans 2:17–29)—consider the deep, insurmountable problems in which all human beings find themselves mired and from which they need rescue, whether they know it or not. Lesson four, "Here's the Solution" (Romans 3:21–31), provides God's solution, and lesson five, "Faith Is the Way" (Romans 4:1–17, 23–25), focuses further on this solution—faith in God's Son, Jesus Christ.

Unit two, "Offering the Best Possible Life," is a study of Romans 5— 8. The lessons in this unit emphasize the benefits of the solution God provides. Lesson six, "It's a Wonderful Life," considers Romans 5:1–11. Lesson seven, "It's a New Way of Life," on Romans 6:1–19, challenges us to live under the Lordship of Christ. Lesson eight, "It's God Life in You," is on Romans 8:1–11 and calls us to consider how God leads us to live lives pleasing to him through God's Spirit who dwells in us. Lesson nine, "It's a Victorious Life," treats Romans 8:12–39 and offers assurance that God's love will always provide for our needs, even in the most difficult times of our lives.

Unit three, "Continuing to Care for the Jewish People," is a one-lesson study of Romans 9—11. These chapters begin with Paul's anguish that his own people had rejected the Christian way. As these chapters conclude, Paul communicated his assured belief that God would continue to care for the Jewish people. The beginning place for understanding these chapters is the likely relationship between the Jewish and Gentile Christians in Rome, a topic with which much of Paul's Letter to the Romans is concerned. Lesson ten is titled "What About the Jewish People?" The question has continuing relevance for us.

Unit four, "Calling for Faithful Living," is on the remaining chapters of Romans, Romans 12—16. These lessons deal with Paul's instructions on how to live in light of the great theological truths of the preceding chapters. Lesson eleven, "Live in Response to God's Mercy," is on Romans 12:1–8. Lesson twelve, "Live Like This," on Romans 12:9— 13:14, offers direction for living the Christian life both in the church and in the world. Lesson thirteen, on Romans 14:1–21, is titled "Welcome Christians with Whom You Disagree." The Roman church needed that lesson, and so do we.

UNIT ONE. PROVIDING THE WAY OUT

Lesson 1	Connecting the Dots	Romans 1:1–17
Lesson 2	No Excuses, No Exceptions	Romans 1:18–32; 2:1–13
Lesson 3	Just Not Good Enough	Romans 2:17–29
Lesson 4	Here's the Solution	Romans 3:21–31

NOTES

1. Thirty or so years earlier, in A.D. 19, Tiberius also had expelled the Jews. See Charles H. Talbert, *Romans*, Smyth and Helwys Bible Commentary (Macon, Georgia: Smyth and Helwys, 2002), 6.
2. Talbert, *Romans*, 12.
3. Unless otherwise indicated, all Scripture quotations are from the New International Version.
4. N. T. Wright, "The Letter to the Romans," *The New Interpreter's Bible*, vol. X (Nashville, Tennessee: Abingdon Press, 2002), paragraph 22 under subhead "The Shape and Theme of Romans" in electronic edition.
5. Talbert, *Romans*, 12.
6. Listing a book does not imply full agreement by the writers or BAPTISTWAY® with all of its comments.

Providing the Way Out

Unit one, "Providing the Way Out," consists of five lessons on Romans 1—4. This unit on the one hand reveals to us the horrible predicament in which we find ourselves under God's judgment, but on the other hand it also reveals to us the wonderful good news of rescue.

Lesson one, "Connecting the Dots" (Romans 1:1–17), comments on the introductory verses of Romans and sets the stage for the rest of the study. The next two lessons—"No Excuses, No Exceptions" (Romans 1:18–32; 2:1–13) and "Just Not Good Enough" (Romans 2:17–29)—consider the insurmountable dilemma in which all people find themselves and from which they need rescue. Lesson four, "Here's the Solution" (Romans 3:21–31), provides God's solution. Lesson five, "Faith Is the Way" (4:1–17, 23–25), focuses further on this solution by reminding us that the answer to everyone's dilemma is to receive God's grace through faith alone. God provides a way out from a dead-end life.[1]

UNIT ONE. PROVIDING THE WAY OUT

Lesson 1	Connecting the Dots	Romans 1:1–17
Lesson 2	No Excuses, No Exceptions	Romans 1:18–32; 2:1–13
Lesson 3	Just Not Good Enough	Romans 2:17–29
Lesson 4	Here's the Solution	Romans 3:21–31
Lesson 5	Faith Is the Way	Romans 4:1–17, 23–25

NOTES

1. Unless otherwise indicated, all Scripture quotations in unit one, lessons one through five, are from the New International Version.

Focal Text

Romans 1:1–17

Background

Romans 1:1–17

Main Idea

The gospel of Jesus Christ offers meaning for all of history and for our lives when we respond by faith.

Question to Explore

How does what God has done in Jesus provide meaning for the events of history and for our lives?

Study Aim

To summarize the meaning of the gospel and state how it provides meaning for the events of history and for our lives

Study and Action Emphases

- Affirm the Bible as our authoritative guide for life and ministry
- Share the gospel with all people
- Develop a growing, vibrant faith
- Value all people as created in the image of God
- Obey and serve Jesus by meeting physical, spiritual, and emotional needs
- Equip people for servant leadership

LESSON ONE

Connecting the Dots

Quick Read

Paul proclaimed that the good news of Jesus Christ fulfilled the promises of the Old Testament and had the power to save people both in the present time and in the future. The gospel reveals God's plan to impart righteousness to people and also reveals what all of history is about.

Rome was the center of the world. At least that is what the ancient Romans thought. In Paul's day it was the center of political power. Rome had consolidated an empire that stretched from present-day England to Iraq. It was the center of military power, with the most successful military the world had ever seen. It was the center of economic power, with trade coming to the city from all over the world. As the old saying went, "All roads lead to Rome." Why shouldn't the Romans have thought that Rome was the center of the world?

In the midst of this powerful city was a little band of Christians. No doubt many of them shared the cultural pride of Rome. But for the most part they were not powerful when compared with the city that surrounded them. Some of them had come straight out of the pagan pool of Gentiles, where they were accustomed to worshiping the gods of the day. Some of these Christians had come from the Jewish faith, where they had known for generations the truth about the one true God. But they had all found another way. They had discovered the wonderful grace of God in his Son Jesus Christ, and they had responded by faith. As they looked around at the power of the world, however, they must have been wondering about the seeming lack of God's power. Where was the power of God in this place?

Paul wrote this letter to the Roman Christians in order to strengthen them and encourage them in their faith. Paul had never been to Rome and had never met the people who made up the church there. In these first few verses, Paul introduced himself to them and thanked God that their faith was making news in churches all over the Roman Empire. But more than that, he gave meaning to their faith. He assured them that since they had responded in faith to the gospel of Christ, their lives had meaning because they were now participating in God's eternal plan for the salvation of the world. God had connected their lives to God's purpose for the history of the whole world, not just the history of Rome.

Romans 1:1–17

1Paul, a servant of Christ Jesus, called to be an apostle and set apart for the gospel of God—**2**the gospel he promised beforehand through his prophets in the Holy Scriptures **3**regarding his Son, who as to his human nature was a descendant of David, **4**and who through the Spirit of holiness was declared with power to be the Son of God by his resurrection from the dead: Jesus Christ our Lord. [5]Through him and for his name's sake, we received grace and apostleship to call people from among all the Gentiles to the obedience that comes from faith. [6]And you also are among those who are called to belong to Jesus Christ.

[7]To all in Rome who are loved by God and called to be saints:

Grace and peace to you from God our Father and from the Lord Jesus Christ.

[8]First, I thank my God through Jesus Christ for all of you, because your faith is being reported all over the world. [9]God, whom I serve with my whole heart in preaching the gospel of his Son, is my witness how constantly I remember you [10]in my prayers at all times; and I pray that now at last by God's will the way may be opened for me to come to you.

[11]I long to see you so that I may impart to you some spiritual gift to make you strong—[12]that is, that you and I may be mutually encouraged by each other's faith. [13]I do not want you to be unaware, brothers, that I planned many times to come to you (but have been prevented from doing so until now) in order that I might have a harvest among you, just as I have had among the other Gentiles.

[14]I am obligated both to Greeks and non-Greeks, both to the wise and the foolish. [15]That is why I am so eager to preach the gospel also to you who are at Rome.

[16]I am not ashamed of the gospel, because it is the power of God for the salvation of everyone who believes: first for the Jew, then for the Gentile. [17]For in the gospel a righteousness from God is revealed, a righteousness that is by faith from first to last, just as it is written: "The righteous will live by faith."

Dear Roman Christians (1:1–7)

When we write a letter we generally start by writing *Dear _____*. We usually don't reveal who is writing the letter until the end, with words like *Sincerely* or *Yours truly*. In Paul's day, however, letters began with the name of the writer, quickly followed by the name of the recipient. Paul followed this format in all of his letters, although in this letter he added considerable substance between his name and the name of the recipients.

Paul began by describing himself as "a servant of Christ Jesus" (Romans 1:1). The word "servant" could also be translated *slave*. The use of this word indicated Paul's total devotion to Christ. He was completely at the disposal of the Lord. The meaning of Paul's life was now completely wrapped up in Jesus. He also said that he had been "called to be an apostle and set apart for the gospel of God" (Rom. 1:1). That means that God had chosen him for a special purpose, and that purpose was to participate in God's purpose for the history of the world.

The gospel was not something new, however. It had been promised and predicted by the testimony of the prophets in the Old Testament. The purpose of God could be traced back to Abraham and the covenant that God made with him in Genesis, as we shall see in Romans 4. In fact, God's purpose was established from the very beginning of the world even before the moment of creation.

The focus of God's purpose is Jesus Christ. Jesus came into this world as a human being, a descendant of King David. But Jesus also came into this world as a divine being, having been revealed as the Son of God by his resurrection. Many people may recognize Jesus as a man in the flesh, but we have not fully understood Jesus until we recognize him as God in the flesh. Jesus was not simply a man who lived on earth for thirty-three years, but he is also God, Lord of all history from beginning to end.

They had discovered the wonderful grace of God in his Son Jesus Christ, and they had responded by faith.

Paul's relationship with the Lord of history gave his life new meaning because he had received God's grace and a mission. God's grace gives undeserved righteousness before God. God's mission for Paul was to call people from among the Gentiles to join with him in God's purpose for the history of the world. Joining that purpose would mean accepting God's grace by faith and achieving God's purpose by obedience that follows faith. If people would join with Paul in God's purpose, it would give new meaning to their lives.

I Want to Come and See You (1:8–15)

Paul gave thanks to God for the Roman Christians. He was thankful because their faith in Christ was making news all over the world. Christians in other parts of the empire must have been encouraged when they learned that people in Rome, the center of the world, were joining God's purpose for the history of the world.

Paul called God as a witness that he prayed constantly for them. Paul knew the importance of the existence of the church in Rome. He wanted

The Righteousness of God

Righteousness is a major theme in the Book of Romans. The term is generally used in reference to being acquitted or justified of wrongdoing in the judicial system. It also may be used in reference to a relationship that has lived up to the expected and previously agreed upon norms.

The phrase "righteousness of God" (Rom. 1:17) can refer to an attribute of God, such as God's justice or God's faithfulness. In this case, God is the subject of righteousness.

The "righteousness of God" can also refer to an activity of God as God establishes what is right and just. God may act to set things right. Indeed, this is what God has done in the gospel. God acted to establish or reestablish rightness and justice in the world.

Finally, the righteousness of God may refer to a status given to the believer. In this case, God is the giver of righteousness as he changes the status of the believer from guilty to not guilty. The term connotes forgiveness and restoration, with the result that we are no longer in a crooked relationship with God. Rather, we are in a right or straight relationship with God. This righteousness comes to the believer solely as a gift of God as a person responds to the gift by faith in Jesus Christ. This usage of "righteousness of God" seems to be the usage in this lesson.

to encourage them with his prayers even as the Roman Christians encouraged Christians all over the world with their faith.

Not only did Paul want to encourage them with his prayers, but also he wanted to encourage them with his presence. He seems to have been praying desperately for an opportunity to visit them in Rome, but for one reason or another he had not been able to do so.

Most of the letters Paul sent were to churches he had started or at least visited. This does not seem to have been the case with the Roman church. We are not sure how the gospel arrived in Rome, but it was not because Paul had been there. Perhaps

> *. . . Since they had responded in faith to the gospel of Christ, their lives had meaning because they were now participating in God's eternal plan for the salvation of the world.*

someone had been converted at Pentecost, had returned to Rome, and had started the Christian movement there. However the gospel arrived in Rome, it does not seem to have been a direct result of Paul's ministry. Nevertheless, Paul wanted to see the Roman Christians so they could encourage each other in the faith.

Paul indicated he wanted to go to Rome for three specific reasons. First, he wanted to impart "some spiritual gift" to them (1:11). The text does not indicate what this gift was. Whatever it was, though, it was sure to be of mutual encouragement. Second, Paul wanted to have a "harvest" among the Romans (1:13). Regardless of the faithfulness of the Roman church, Paul knew that still thousands on thousands of people needed to be invited into the purpose of God. Finally, Paul said he wanted "to preach the gospel" to them (1:15). Although the Christians there had heard and accepted God's grace, they had not heard Paul preach. He wanted the opportunity to speak the good news to them and to encourage them in the faith.

> ... God had chosen him for a special purpose, and that purpose was to participate in God's purpose for the history of the world.

Paul had tried to visit them before but had been prevented from doing so. He did not indicate what had hindered him, but perhaps he had been busy elsewhere or had been hindered by persecution.

Paul noted that his mission from God obligated him to preach to both "Greeks and non-Greeks." The word translated "non-Greeks" in the New International Version is translated "barbarians" in other versions (NRSV, NASB, KJV). Barbarians were Gentiles who spoke a language other than Greek. To Greek speakers, their language sounded like babbling, and the people seemed foolish. Barbarians were people from the northern lands that later became Germany. These people generally were hated by the Romans. Nevertheless, Paul was obligated to invite them into God's purpose for the world as well. The gospel of Jesus Christ is a universal gospel because it is God's purpose for the history of the whole world. Barbarians were living in Rome. If Paul could preach to them, the gospel could spread among their people as well.

Here Is the Point (1:16–17)

These verses reveal the point of the whole letter to the Romans. In fact, these verses reveal the point of all of life and history itself.

The point is that the power of God (even in a powerful city like Rome) is revealed in the gospel of Jesus Christ because the gospel reveals that righteousness before God is achieved by faith by everyone who believes. Political power, military might, or economic strength does not indicate

Case Study

Your materialistic friend expresses dismay at the futility of life, saying, "I have worked and worked to get ahead in life. I have made a lot of money and have been successful in my job. But now that I have reached my goals I have nothing else to live for. What is the point of all I have achieved?" What would you say to this person?

true power. True power in life and in all of history from the beginning to the end is revealed in the gospel of Jesus that Paul proclaimed.

I have always found it strange that Paul had to assert that he was "not ashamed of the gospel" (1:16). Why would he assume anyone would think he was "ashamed"? One reason might be that the gospel relies on the life and death of a simple carpenter from an insignificant little country at the outskirts of the empire. Too, this person, Jesus of Nazareth, died the humiliating death of a criminal at the hands of powerful leaders and Roman might. Where is the power in that? Staking one's life on that kind of weakness seems foolish when compared to the powers of this world. Enslaving oneself, as Paul had done, to a crucified carpenter seemed idiotic. Yet Paul proudly proclaimed the gospel.

> *True power in life and in all of history from the beginning to the end is revealed in the gospel of Jesus that Paul proclaimed.*

The true meaning of life and history is in the gospel because it provides the power of God for the salvation of all people and all of creation. The gospel makes things right because the gospel reveals how to be right with God. The gospel reveals God's purpose and gives meaning to all of life and history.

The point is that God desires people to be righteous. That does not mean *self*-righteous. "Righteous" is a legal term derived from the law court. It refers to a new status for people. We might imagine a judge declaring innocence upon a defendant, not because the defendant is innocent, but because the judge is merciful and gracious. When a judge declares a person not guilty, the

> *The gospel reveals God's purpose and gives meaning to all of life and history.*

person's status is changed. The defendant now has a clean record and is back in right relationship with society. When God declares us righteous,

God is declaring a new status on us. Our guilt is forgiven, and we are in a right relationship with God.

This "righteousness" is received by faith. Paul quoted the Old Testament prophet Habakkuk as his overall text for the Letter to the Romans: "The righteous will live by faith" (Rom. 1:17; Habakkuk 2:4). We will see this theme over and over again in the Letter to the Romans. Life that has meaning in God's purpose for the history of the world is a life of faith, not of might. If we trust in the things that seem powerful in this world, we will ultimately find our lives meaningless. But if we trust in a crucified God, a God who seems weak in this world, we will ultimately find the meaning of life and all of history.

> . . . *The center of the universe is found at the cross of Christ.*

The Romans thought Rome was the center of the world. The truth is, the center of the universe is found at the cross of Christ. It is the power of God for salvation.

Implications and Actions

As you read these words today, you find yourself on a blue and brown sphere we call earth, floating in space. There are stars that are billions on billions of miles away, and more stars in galaxies that are so distant our minds cannot comprehend it all. Such a thought can make our lives seem insignificant. Why are we here?

We are here because God has declared his purpose of making things right. We are here because God is inviting us to join with him in the eternal flow of history as it moves toward the final salvation of creation. When we respond to God's gracious offer by faith in Jesus Christ, our purpose becomes clear, and our lives have meaning.

> *Life that has meaning in God's purpose for the history of the world is a life of faith, not of might.*

If we search, though, for meaning in the things that seem powerful in this world, we will be disappointed. We love our country. If, though, we trust in our country for meaning because we think it is the center of the world, we will find we have missed our purpose. We may trust money to give us meaning. But watch out for that! Money can be blown away in the next downturn of the Dow. Then where will our purpose be? No, the things that seem powerful in this world do not stack up to the power of God crucified. The center of the world is at the cross.

QUESTIONS

1. What are some of the powerful things in this world that people trust to provide meaning in life?

2. Do you find it a difficult concept that God's power is usually revealed in ways that seem weak in this world?

3. What do you think it means when the lesson says that the gospel offers meaning for all of history?

4. How has the gospel provided meaning for your life?

Focal Text

Romans 1:18–32; 2:1–13

Background

Romans 1:18—2:16

Main Idea

All people—the "religious" as well as the "sinners"—are without excuse before God and stand in need of God's grace.

Question to Explore

So why am I—as good as I am—without excuse before God?

Study Aim

To summarize why both "religious" people and blatant "sinners" are without excuse before God and stand in need of God's grace

Study and Action Emphases

- Affirm the Bible as our authoritative guide for life and ministry
- Share the gospel with all people
- Develop a growing, vibrant faith
- Value all people as created in the image of God

LESSON TWO

No Excuses, No Exceptions

Quick Read

Paul delivered some bad news. The bad news is that all people stand under the wrath of God. No matter who you are, you have no excuse to use when God judges you, and there are no exceptions to the rule. But there is good news too.

27

My heart always skips a beat when someone begins a conversation like this: *What do you want to hear first, the good news or the bad news?* I get nervous because it is clear that bad news is coming. Too, I am always afraid that whatever the good news is, it will not be good enough to make up for the bad news. Nevertheless, I always ask for the bad news first and hope the bad news is not as bad as it could be and the good news that follows is better than I hoped for.

When Paul wrote to the Romans, he had good news and bad news. He did not give his readers a chance to decide which news they got first. He unloaded the bad news first. And, no doubt about it; the bad news is bad. In fact, it is about as bad as news can get.

Romans 1:18–32

18The wrath of God is being revealed from heaven against all the godlessness and wickedness of men who suppress the truth by their wickedness, **19**since what may be known about God is plain to them, because God has made it plain to them. **20**For since the creation of the world God's invisible qualities—his eternal power and divine nature—have been clearly seen, being understood from what has been made, so that men are without excuse.

21For although they knew God, they neither glorified him as God nor gave thanks to him, but their thinking became futile and their foolish hearts were darkened. **22**Although they claimed to be wise, they became fools **23**and exchanged the glory of the immortal God for images made to look like mortal man and birds and animals and reptiles.

24Therefore God gave them over in the sinful desires of their hearts to sexual impurity for the degrading of their bodies with one another. **25**They exchanged the truth of God for a lie, and worshiped and served created things rather than the Creator—who is forever praised. Amen.

26Because of this, God gave them over to shameful lusts. Even their women exchanged natural relations for unnatural ones. **27**In the same way the men also abandoned natural relations with women and were inflamed with lust for one another. Men committed indecent acts with other men, and received in themselves the due penalty for their perversion.

28Furthermore, since they did not think it worthwhile to retain the knowledge of God, he gave them over to a depraved mind, to do what ought not to be done. **29**They have become filled with every kind of wickedness, evil, greed and depravity. They are full of envy, murder, strife, deceit and malice. They are gossips, **30**slanderers, God-haters, insolent, arrogant and boastful; they invent ways of doing evil; they disobey their parents; **31**they are senseless, faithless, heartless, ruthless. **32**Although they know God's righteous decree that those who do such things deserve death, they not only continue to do these very things but also approve of those who practice them.

Romans 2:1–13

1You, therefore, have no excuse, you who pass judgment on someone else, for at whatever point you judge the other, you are condemning yourself, because you who pass judgment do the same things. **2**Now we know that God's judgment against those who do such things is based on truth. **3**So when you, a mere man, pass judgment on them and yet do the same things, do you think you will escape God's judgment? **4**Or do you show contempt for the riches of his kindness, tolerance and patience, not realizing that God's kindness leads you toward repentance?

5But because of your stubbornness and your unrepentant heart, you are storing up wrath against yourself for the day of God's wrath, when his righteous judgment will be revealed. **6**God "will give to each person according to what he has done." **7**To those who by persistence in doing good seek glory, honor and immortality, he will give eternal life. **8**But for those who are self-seeking and who reject the truth and follow evil, there will be wrath and anger. **9**There will be trouble and distress for every human being who does evil: first for the Jew, then for the Gentile; **10**but glory, honor and peace for everyone who does good: first for the Jew, then for the Gentile. **11**For God does not show favoritism.

12All who sin apart from the law will also perish apart from the law, and all who sin under the law will be judged by the law. **13**For it is not those who hear the law who are righteous in God's sight, but it is those who obey the law who will be declared righteous.

The Bad News Is Really Bad (1:18–32)

The bad news is about as bad as it can get. Paul wrote, "The wrath of God is being revealed. . . ." No news is worse than that! I have to admit that "wrath of God" language always makes me a little nervous. When I hear about the wrath of God, I have images of street preachers carrying signs and accosting pedestrians on city streets with vile preachments that condemn ordinary men and women to the sulfur and brimstone of hell. I question the effectiveness of those particular evangelistic strategies, but I suppose such actions speak the truth in many ways. "The wrath of God is being revealed" to you, they shout.

> I always ask for the bad news first and hope the bad news is not as bad as it could be and the good news that follows is better than I hoped for.

Another image that may come to mind is Hurricane Katrina. Some preachers immediately announced that Katrina was God's wrath being revealed on a sinful city. I am uncomfortable about assigning God's wrath to hurricanes, earthquakes, tsunamis, and such. But after reading what Paul said, perhaps we wonder.

Of course, God's wrath is not that hard to understand when you take a look at the human condition. A person doesn't have to be a Bible scholar to see that people are sinners.

Paul began his indictment of sinners by writing about Gentiles, who had no special revelation from God. These were folks from the pagan world who had not had the advantage of knowing God's law. They were guilty because of their godlessness and wickedness, by which they had intentionally suppressed the truth (Romans 1:18). However, even they should have known better than to do the things they did. Even they knew there was a God, even if they didn't know much about God.

How did they know? The natural world revealed God to them. A person may have never read the Ten Commandments or any other part of the Bible. Yet the person knows that murder, rape, and stealing are wrong. The Gentiles Paul was talking about had no excuse before God because it was obvious to even the most casual observer that they were sinners.

> The good news is better than the bad news is bad!

Paul gave a list of examples from his world, and the list doesn't sound much different from our world. The main problem was that even though the natural world made it obvious there was a God, the Gentiles had a habit of exchanging the Creator for the creation. This practice was an example of their foolishness. Paul gave three examples of this sinful exchange.

First, they exchanged the immortal God for images of mortal creatures and worshiped them as if they were God (Romans 1:21–23). This is idolatry. Idolatry is the essence of the human predicament and leads to every other kind of immorality. Exchanging the Creator for the created is the height of foolishness.

Therefore, God's wrath is expressed by the terrible phrase, "God gave them over. . . " (Rom. 1:24, 26, 28). In other words, God allowed them to continue down the path of destruction. I almost picture God throwing up his hands in resignation and giving them up to what they had chosen.

The practice of exchanging the Creator for the creation then led them to other sinful desires. Once you have exchanged the Creator for the creation, there is no reason not to worship other things God created. One example Paul pointed out was the abandonment of all sexual restraint.

The bad news is about as bad as it can get.

Sexual immorality is simply the extension of idolatry because it means exchanging the eternal will of the Creator for our own temporary desires for the created (1:24).

Second, they exchanged the truth of God for a lie, which also made the sin of idolatry even worse (1:25). Once again, God gave them over to their own desires. Again the result of this idolatry is expressed in sexual terms. Paul said that the result was not only heterosexual immorality but also homosexual immorality. Exchanging God's truth for the world's lies will always lead us down a path of destruction.

In verse 28 Paul implied that the third idolatrous exchange was exchanging knowledge of God for willful ignorance of God. All of creation was pointing to God, but people were convinced that knowledge of God was not worth their time. Once again, "God gave them over. . . ."

Paul then unleashed a torrent of words that name sins resulting from willful ignorance of God. Those who exchanged the Creator for the creation became filled with "wickedness, evil, greed and depravity" (1:29). They were "full of envy, murder, strife, deceit and malice" (1:29). Paul continued to recite a list of vices that result when people forget God.

Isn't is interesting that sins that we usually think of as minor sins like gossip, parental disobedience, and envy are in the same list as murder and depravity? Paul said that people who do these things "deserve death" (1:32)!

The bad news is that the wrath of God is being revealed. Paul referred in these verses to the Gentiles, who had no knowledge of God except for what they could see in the natural world. But that should have been enough for them to refuse to exchange the Creator for the creation. Therefore, they were guilty and under God's wrath. The bad news is really bad.

General and Special Revelation

Theologians speak of the doctrine of revelation when they are discussing ways that God reveals himself to us. The doctrine is usually expressed in two ways. Paul discussed both of these ways in Romans 1:18—2:16.

The first way to discuss this doctrine is called *general revelation*. General revelation is God's revealing himself to us through nature. The psalmist proclaimed, "The heavens declare the glory of God" (Psalm 19:1). This kind of revelation is available to anyone and everyone. General revelation does not tell us much about God, except that God is the Creator, but it should make us aware of God's existence.

The second way to discuss revelation is called *special revelation*. Special revelation is God's intervening in a special way to reveal himself to people. God has intervened in history through his mighty acts recorded in Scripture. Scripture itself reveals the nature of God and instructs us of God's demands and expectations. God spoke through prophets and continues to use the preached word through the power of the Holy Spirit. But the greatest revelation of God is Jesus Christ. In Jesus we have the exact image of God (Hebrews 1:3). Those who have special revelation have the advantage of understanding God in a special way. With this knowledge comes responsibility.

The Bad News Gets Worse (2:1–11)

Now Paul turned his attention to the Jews. For them the news was even worse because they had received special revelation from God. They had the Old Testament law, the traditions of the Jewish community, and their faith in the one true God. When you have special advantages like that, it is easy to look at others who are less advantaged and judge them. Yet Paul said that when the Jews judged the sins of the Gentiles, they were really condemning themselves because they had done the same things. Even with the special knowledge of God that they had, they were as guilty as the pagans, if not more so.

We know what God wants, and yet we disobey him anyway.

Verses 6–10 may seem to suggest that Paul said that the way of salvation is related to good works. In a sense, Paul did argue that if one can perfectly keep the law the result will be "eternal life" (2:7). But later, Paul will remind us that no one keeps the law; therefore, the law is good only for pointing out our sin to us. The law makes us aware of our sin because it tells us what God expects (see 3:20–23).

Paul's words in 2:1–11 have special significance for people who seem to be religious. When we who think of ourselves as religious quit looking around in the world and turn around to look at ourselves, we may see that we are the biggest sinners of all! After all, God has told us what sin is, and yet we go right ahead and do it anyway. We are not like those folks out there in the world who have no clue about the Bible, Jesus, or the Holy Spirit. Many of us grew up in church learning right and wrong from our earliest days in Sunday School. We know what God wants, and yet we disobey him anyway.

Only when we grasp how bad the bad news is can we have real appreciation for the good news of Jesus.

Of course, we may avoid what seem to be the really big sins. We generally don't murder people or hold up banks. No, our sin likely is more subtle. We are told not to be greedy, lustful, unkind, or gossips. We are not supposed to be prejudiced, arrogant, slanderers, or judgmental. Yet, there we sit in church—guilty.

The bad news just got worse. It is understandable that the wrath of God is deserved by sinners out in the world. After all, natural instinct ought to make them know better. But it is also a fact that we who claim to be religious stand under God's wrath as well. We know what God expects of us because it has been revealed to us in the Bible and the Holy Spirit convicts us. But we sin anyway.

It's Bad News All Around (2:12–13)

All human beings stand under the wrath of God because all human beings are hopelessly entangled in sin. Some people are guilty because even if they know nothing about the Bible or the Ten Commandments, they know by nature that some things are right and some things are wrong. They will be judged accordingly.

Exchanging God's truth for the world's lies will always lead us down a path of destruction.

Others of us are guilty because we know exactly what God expects of us. We have read the Bible, and the Holy Spirit convinces us of what is right. Yet we do the very things that are the opposite of

Case Study

You are trying to determine whether God wants you to be a missionary to people who have never heard of Jesus or had any access to a Bible or other Christian witness. If you go and tell them about Jesus, you will be sharing knowledge of God with them that will demand a change of lifestyle. They worship their own gods in ignorance. Would it be better to just leave them in ignorance or to tell them the truth with the risk that they will reject Christ?

what we know. The point is that all people—the "religious" as well as the "sinners"—are without excuse before God and stand in need of God's grace.

Sin is the dominating, ruling force in the human experience. We are all hopelessly entangled in sin, standing under the wrath of God. The bad news is really bad.

The Good News Is Better

Finally, we get to the good news. The good news is better than the bad news is bad! It does not always work out that way in our world.

For example, a lawyer told his client, "We've just gotten your test results back, and I have some good news and some bad news." The client asked for the bad news first. "The bad news is that your DNA matched the blood that was all over the crime scene." The client asked what the good news was. His attorney replied, "The good news is that your cholesterol is down to 130!"

The good news didn't match the bad news, did it? In God's world, though, even though the bad news is really bad, the good news is always better than the bad news is bad.

Paul does not expound on the good news until Romans 3:21. But he has given us a hint of it in Romans 1:16–17. Paul may have made a big deal about the wrath of God being "revealed" (1:18), but the good news he has already stated is that the righteousness of God has been "revealed" in Jesus Christ (1:17). Furthermore, when the Roman Christians first read these words, they already knew about the cross of Christ. We too live on this side of the cross. We can look back and know that even though the bad news is bad, the good news is better than the bad news is bad.

The good news is that Jesus Christ rescues us from the wrath of God. In this world, the bad news is news of death, but the good news is news of resurrection! In this world the bad news is news of grief, but the good news provides peace. In this world the bad news is that all of us are sinners, but the good news is the message of forgiveness and hope. The good news is better than the bad news is bad!

Implications and Actions

Can you begin to understand why we needed to hear the bad news first? Only when we grasp how bad the bad news is can we have real appreciation for the good news of Jesus.

I don't like looking at myself and discovering that I am a hopeless sinner. Only, though, when I realize what a predicament I am in am I able to be truly thankful for the good news.

The good news is what keeps us coming to worship week after week. Worship helps us express our relief and gratitude to God for rescuing us from wrath. We sing songs of praise, not out of duty or habit, but out of gratitude for rescue. We give money, not because it is church fund-raising or out of a sense of buying God's favor, but out of thanksgiving to God for plucking us out of a preposterous predicament.

We need to know the bad news first so that when the good news comes we will give thanks. Even though the bad news is really bad, the good news is better. Praise the Lord!

QUESTIONS

1. How would you define the wrath of God?

2. How do you know whether something is God's wrath or just a natural occurrence?

3. What do you think about God's wrath as simply God giving people over to self-destruction (Rom. 1:24, 26, 28)?

4. Do you ever find yourself judging other people who may not have the same spiritual background you have?

5. What is worse in God's eyes—sexual sin or greed, envy, and gossip?

6. What do you think about the theological assertion that all sins are the result of idolatry? In other words, sin is a result of exchanging the Creator for the created.

Focal Text
Romans 2:17–29

Background
Romans 2:17—3:20

Main Idea
Right relationship with God must be based on a relationship of the heart rather than on external religious identity and actions.

Question to Explore
Do you rely on religious identity, rituals, and behavior or on a genuine relationship with God?

Study Aim
To analyze whether I am seeking to be related to God through a genuine relationship or through religious identity and rituals

Study and Action Emphases
- Affirm the Bible as our authoritative guide for life and ministry
- Share the gospel with all people
- Develop a growing, vibrant faith
- Value all people as created in the image of God

LESSON THREE

Just Not Good Enough

Quick Read
Religious ritual may be helpful. Righteous perfection is a nice but unrealistic goal. What a person really needs is a relationship with the living God. A relationship changes one's heart.

Here's a question that you are probably not asked every day: *How religious are you?* A recent poll concluded that for the most part Americans are a very religious people. A whopping nine out of ten Americans believe there is a God in some form or fashion. Sixty percent of the people polled said that they pray often, and more than half said that religion was very important to their lives. Now that does not mean that everyone understands God or faith the way Christians do, but it does indicate that by and large Americans are a religious people.[1]

I would suspect that if asked the same questions, most of us would identify ourselves as being religious people. After all, you are reading this Bible study presumably in preparation for a Sunday School class, a decidedly religious thing to do. I myself have been known to be a religious person, not surprisingly, I suppose, since I am a Baptist preacher. My dad was a minister before me, and so I was in church from before I was born. I have been to seminary and divinity school, I tithe more than ten percent of my income, and I participate in the rituals and traditions of the faith.

Perhaps you could also give similar testimonies of religiosity. You have been baptized, you show up for Sunday School and worship, and you give to the Lord's work. If anyone were to ask you whether you were a religious person, likely you could rightly answer in the affirmative.

Unfortunately, all of that is just not good enough.

Romans 2:17–29

[17]Now you, if you call yourself a Jew; if you rely on the law and brag about your relationship to God; [18]if you know his will and approve of what is superior because you are instructed by the law; [19]if you are convinced that you are a guide for the blind, a light for those who are in the dark, [20]an instructor of the foolish, a teacher of infants, because you have in the law the embodiment of knowledge and truth—[21]you, then, who teach others, do you not teach yourself? You who preach against stealing, do you steal? [22]You who say that people should not commit adultery, do you commit adultery? You who abhor idols, do you rob temples? [23]You who brag about the law, do you dishonor God by breaking the law? [24]As it is written: "God's name is blasphemed among the Gentiles because of you."

[25]Circumcision has value if you observe the law, but if you break the law, you have become as though you had not been circumcised. [26]If those who are not circumcised keep the law's requirements, will they

not be regarded as though they were circumcised? **27**The one who is not circumcised physically and yet obeys the law will condemn you who, even though you have the written code and circumcision, are a lawbreaker.

28A man is not a Jew if he is only one outwardly, nor is circumcision merely outward and physical. **29**No, a man is a Jew if he is one inwardly; and circumcision is circumcision of the heart, by the Spirit, not by the written code. Such a man's praise is not from men, but from God.

The Problem of Privilege (2:17–24)

Paul said that the decidedly religious Jews, of which he himself was one, had a problem. They were called out as the people of God; they understood and relied on the Jewish law; and they bragged to the world about their special relationship with the Lord.[2] They claimed to know God's will both for themselves and for others because they had received special revelation from God when God gave the law to Moses.

This special privilege of the Jewish people gave them the prerogative and the responsibility of providing light to those who lived in spiritual darkness and teaching those who were spiritually immature. However, Paul said, they had fallen short of their responsibility by failing themselves to live up to the knowledge they had.

The rhetorical questions in Romans 2:21–22 were designed to entrap the critics of Paul's argument. He accused them of stealing, committing adultery, and robbing temples. It is not clear why Paul used these particular accusations against the religious Jews, but perhaps he knew something that we do not. These accusations exposed those who had made the lofty claims of religious privilege as being hypocritical—failing to practice what they preached. In other words, Paul argued that all privileges are meaningless if one does not respond to them with sincere and constant obedience.

We must be careful here not to read into this text any hint of anti-Semitism. After all, Paul himself, not to mention Jesus, was a Jew. The problem was not Jewishness. The problem was that the people who were privileged with special knowledge did not live up to the knowledge they had. The problem was disobedience.

This hypocrisy resulted in outsiders (Gentiles) ridiculing the name of God. God had chosen Israel to deliver God's message of salvation to the entire world. However, the disobedience of Israel by the breaking of God's law was resulting in ridicule and blasphemy. The privilege of special knowledge had been abused, and the privilege had become a problem.

When Religion Goes Wrong (2:25–27)

Paul then mentioned a particular religious ritual that the Jews practiced. The ritual of circumcision had a long history within the Jewish tradition and was a sign of the covenant God had made with Abraham. Circumcision marked a person as being a part of the covenant community of Israel. The Jews seem to have assumed that it guaranteed the blessing of God on them.

Yet Paul said that circumcision was of no spiritual value to anyone unless the person perfectly kept the law. The common thought was that the circumcised could not be lost and the uncircumcised could not be saved. Paul reversed this belief by saying that not only does disobedience endanger the salvation circumcised people thought they had, but obedience to the Lord would bring salvation to the uncircumcised. The ritual practice of circumcision was no guarantee of escape from the wrath of God.

. . . Practicing the rituals of religion is not good enough.

So does that mean something is wrong with participating in religious rituals, whether the ritual is circumcision or any other ritual we may practice? Of course not. Christians practice all sorts of rituals, among them baptism and the Lord's Supper. There is nothing wrong in practicing the rituals of religion. In fact, I believe the rituals of religion are very important for our spiritual well-being.

. . . The people who were privileged with special knowledge did not live up to the knowledge they had.

After all, rituals mean something, don't they? In the ritual of baptism we see a powerful reenactment of the crucifixion and resurrection as well as a symbol of the new believer's conversion experience. In the Lord's Supper we are reminded again and again of the sacrifice of Jesus on the cross. Other traditional rituals serve to tie us to believers of the past and teach faith to believers of the future. Something important happens when we practice the rituals of religion.

But practicing the rituals of religion is not good enough. Our relationship with God does not rely on how well we practice religious rituals.

Baptism is an important ritual, but being baptized does not make you right with God any more than swimming in the ocean makes you a fish. Being a member of the church is valuable, but it does not save you. God is not calling for ritual; God is calling for righteousness.

Cutting to the Heart of the Matter (2:28–29)

God is calling for perfect righteousness that is achieved by perfect obedience! However, out of all of the religious people I have ever known, some of whom are quite accomplished in the practice of religious rituals, I have never known anyone who was completely righteous. There are no perfect people regardless of how religious a person may be.

> *God is not calling for ritual; God is calling for righteousness.*

I recently learned about a punk rock band that has just released a new album. The name of the band is *No One Is*

Circumcision in Jewish Culture and the Early Church

In Israel, circumcision was performed on male babies, generally on the eighth day after birth. Since the time of Abraham it had been a sign of the special covenant between God and God's chosen people (see Genesis 17).

This rite became symbolic of being a part of a chosen people of God. By New Testament times circumcision was seen as an indispensable mark of a relationship with God. First-century Jews assumed it was impossible for the uncircumcised to be in right relationship with God.

The Judaizers continually challenged the early church. They were Jewish Christians who advocated that salvation was not only dependent on grace through faith but also on obedience to the law of Moses, which included circumcision.

The Apostle Paul led the church, particularly at the Jerusalem Council (Acts 15), to remove circumcision as an assumed requirement for salvation. Paul argued that salvation was by God's grace through faith alone, and not because of any rite or ritual, including circumcision.

Perfect. They are right! No one is perfect, and most of us don't even have to try to live up to it. We are just naturally imperfect.

I must confess that in my own life, as religious as I am, perfection has eluded me for a long time now. I remember sitting in church one day when I was a child and determining that from that moment on I was going to be perfect. I would obey all of the commandments, I would think only about God, and I would listen intently to sermons. Ten minutes later I found myself daydreaming about football right in the middle of the sermon! Oh well, I tried.

While ritual may change us on the outside, a relationship changes us on the inside.

You may have tried to be perfect as well. You would never covet your neighbor's property; you always are going to help those in need; you are going to shake off those old feelings of prejudice; and you are going to be perfect with absolute humility. Then ten minutes later you catch yourself thinking about how to get a bigger boat than your neighbor just got, or you are dreaming up some plan for revenge against someone, and your perfection has gone out the window. Oh well, you tried.

We all know it is true. No matter how religious we are on the outside, no one is truly righteous on the inside.

Paul argued that we can be religious on the outside, but it doesn't do any good until God has cut into our hearts with the power of his Spirit. Perfect righteousness is impossible. Religious ritual, as helpful as it is, is not enough. What we need is relationship. While ritual may change us on the outside, a relationship changes us on the inside. Righteous perfection always ends up in a frustrating failure of the flesh, but a relationship cuts to the heart of the matter.

The deeper our love grows and the more we get to know God, the more God changes us on both the inside and the outside.

The heart of the matter is that we are dependent on God to change us on the inside through a relationship with God through Jesus Christ. Relationship changes the heart.

Think about a relationship that you have had that has changed your heart. If you are married, the obvious relationship would be with your spouse. Do you remember how your heart changed when you met your spouse? The deeper your love grows the more you are changed. The change begins on the inside, but soon the change that has occurred on the inside results in changes on the outside as well. The change in your heart comes because you have a relationship with someone.

Case Study

Your eight-year-old child comes to you and announces that she wants to be baptized. How would you talk to her concerning the difference between the ritual of baptism and a relationship with God? How would you talk to her to determine whether her desire for baptism is a valid response to faith in Jesus or a desire to "join the church" as her friends have done?

That is what it is like when you have a relationship with God. When we meet God through Jesus Christ, God changes our heart. God molds us, shapes us, and even cuts out the parts of our heart that are unclean. The deeper our love grows and the more we get to know God, the more God changes us on both the inside and the outside. God cuts away the things he doesn't want in us and changes us forever.

Religious ritual may be helpful. Righteous perfection is a nice but unrealistic goal. What a person really needs is a relationship with the living God. A relationship changes one's heart.

God Is Still Faithful (3:1–20)

There is an advantage for people who have special revelation from God and not just general revelation in nature.[3] Israel, for example, did have knowledge of God from the law, and that knowledge had led them to certain religious practices.

The problem was that Israel, just like all of us, was unfaithful to the covenant God made with them. Nevertheless, God is still faithful, and God's grace is especially evident even when we are unfaithful. God's grace does not, of course, mean that we should sin in order to force God to pour out more grace on us. Paul quickly denounced that proposition. No matter what we do, though, we know that God continues to want a relationship with us.

What really counts is a relationship with God.

The sad fact is that all of us are sinners. Whether we are Jews or Gentiles, men or women, rich or poor—all of us fall short of God's purpose. We cannot be perfect. God, however, makes it possible for us to be righteous, not by ritual or privilege, but by relationship.

Implications and Actions

We are a religious people. I am thankful for the religious heritage that has been handed down to us from our ancestors. I am grateful for the traditions and rituals that help us to express our faith. The rituals of our religion are important because they remind us of the truths of our faith and help us teach the faith to our children.

We can have a relationship with God when we put our faith in Jesus Christ.

But when you cut to the heart of the matter, practicing religious ritual is not enough. Rituals like baptism, the Lord's Supper, church membership, and so on, are outward expressions of religion, but they do not necessarily indicate that we have a changed heart. What really counts is a relationship with God. That relationship changes our heart.

We can have a relationship with God when we put our faith in Jesus Christ. As that relationship grows, it penetrates deeper and deeper into our lives, changing us from the inside out.

QUESTIONS

1. What are some of the rituals we practice when we express our faith? Do you think that rituals get in the way of a relationship with God, or is our relationship with God enhanced by the rituals?

2. What did Paul mean when he used the image "circumcision of the heart" (2:29)?

3. Do you think it is important to be a member of a church? Or is a decision to follow Christ without church membership enough for mature Christian discipleship? In other words, does church membership have any benefit for the believer, or is it simply a ritual with little or no spiritual benefit?

4. What is the place of religious rituals, religious traditions, and religious experiences in a relationship with God?

NOTES

1. www.PollingReport.com, Gallup poll, May 2–4, 2004; accessed 11/06/2006.
2. See Philippians 3:4–6 for Paul's accomplishments as a Jew.
3. See the small article, "General and Special Revelation," in lesson two.

Focal Text

Romans 3:21–31

Background

Romans 3:21–31

Main Idea

God has provided graciously in Christ a way of rescue for all people through their faith.

Question to Explore

How can people get out of the mess they—we—are in?

Study Aim

To consider how people are saved and to affirm or reaffirm my faith in what God has done in Christ for me

Study and Action Emphases

- Affirm the Bible as our authoritative guide for life and ministry
- Share the gospel with all people
- Develop a growing, vibrant faith
- Value all people as created in the image of God

LESSON FOUR

Here's the Solution

Quick Read

Since we are all sinners, we all find ourselves in the direst of circumstances, under the wrath of God. However, God revealed that we could be rescued from wrath by receiving God's righteousness through faith in Jesus Christ.

Every human being is in dire straits when it comes to being righteous before God. Paul made that clear in Romans 1:18—3:20. Paul has, in no uncertain terms, pronounced God's wrath on all people, whether they are Jews or Gentiles. Is there any hope? If there is hope, how can we be rescued from such desperate circumstances?

Do we need to subject ourselves to various rituals, even to the point of torturing our bodies? Is that the kind of thing God needs for us to be righteous before him? Do we need to resort to such practices before God will rescue us from the desperate situation in which we find ourselves? We can be thankful that God has provided a better way.

Romans 3:21–31

[21] But now a righteousness from God, apart from law, has been made known, to which the Law and the Prophets testify. [22] This righteousness from God comes through faith in Jesus Christ to all who believe. There is no difference, [23] for all have sinned and fall short of the glory of God, [24] and are justified freely by his grace through the redemption that came by Christ Jesus. [25] God presented him as a sacrifice of atonement, through faith in his blood. He did this to demonstrate his justice, because in his forbearance he had left the sins committed beforehand unpunished— [26] he did it to demonstrate his justice at the present time, so as to be just and the one who justifies those who have faith in Jesus.

[27] Where, then, is boasting? It is excluded. On what principle? On that of observing the law? No, but on that of faith. [28] For we maintain that a man is justified by faith apart from observing the law. [29] Is God the God of Jews only? Is he not the God of Gentiles too? Yes, of Gentiles too, [30] since there is only one God, who will justify the circumcised by faith and the uncircumcised through that same faith. [31] Do we, then, nullify the law by this faith? Not at all! Rather, we uphold the law.

The Rescue Is Revealed (3:21–22a)

In Romans 3:20, Paul made clear that we cannot receive God's righteousness by obeying the law. Neither is receiving God's righteousness simply a matter of being born into the right family or nation. We can be thankful, too, that righteousness is not attained by engaging in various ritualistic practices. In fact, Paul has emphasized that rescue from our dilemma cannot be achieved by our own efforts.

If we cannot achieve righteousness ourselves, how then are we rescued? Verse 22 states the answer: "through faith in Jesus Christ." We are saved because God has revealed that he will freely rescue us when we accept his gift of grace through faith.

This was a new concept. The words "but now" at the beginning of verse 21 indicate that God has revealed a whole new paradigm for how one is righteous before God. People had always thought *they* had to do something to earn God's righteousness. But now it has been revealed that it was *God* who did something to make it possible for us to be rescued.

The Old Testament ("the Law and the Prophets") had hinted at this concept, but now this new paradigm has been fully revealed by God in the gospel. This new paradigm for righteousness does not replace "the Law and the Prophets," but in Jesus we see clearly what "the Law and the Prophets" were teaching.

These verses get us to the main point of Romans. Faith is the only basis for salvation.

Many people think faith is the same thing as intellectual belief. But faith is deeper than belief. For example, I can go to the airport and believe that a huge hunk of metal can lift off the ground and deposit me safely anywhere in the world. I can stand at the gate; I can have belief that the pilot knows how to fly the plane; and I may even recommend to other people that they should fly in a plane because I believe in my head that flying is a safe way to travel. But it is not real faith until I, myself, get on the plane and trust the plane and the pilot to fly.

> *If we cannot achieve righteousness ourselves, how then are we rescued?*

Faith is giving up all control to someone else and trusting the one in whom you have placed your faith to get you to the right place. Faith is placing your life in someone else's hands.

Faith in Jesus is more than just intellectual belief. It is placing your life in God's hands and trusting God to get you to the right destination. Faith says, *I will go wherever you take me, and I will trust that you will take care of me.*

Children have this kind of faith. Young children generally don't worry about how they are going to eat today, or where they are going to get clothes. They just trust that mom and dad are going to take care of them.

Verses 21–22a deliver an important message. Righteousness comes to those who place their faith in Jesus and trust that Jesus is going to get them to the right destination.

Everyone Is Rescued in the Same Way (3:22b–25a)

Paul reiterated that everyone, whether Jew or Gentile, was in the same dilemma and would be rescued by God in the same way. There is not one way for Jews to be saved and another way for Gentiles to be saved. All are saved only by God's grace when they receive that grace in faith.

The reason for this is that all people, both Jew and Gentile, are sinners. Paul had made this thought abundantly clear in his previous discussion. In verse 23 he said it again, "For all have sinned and fall short of the glory of God." Therefore, since all have sinned in the same way, all are rescued in the same way.

Verses 24–25 contain some important words that beg for explanation. They give us images that help us understand what rescue from sin is like.

First is the word "justified." This word is a legal term that denotes a change of status from one who is guilty to one who is innocent. With the recent advent of DNA testing, some people who had been convicted of crimes have had their convictions overturned. Their status before the court has changed from guilty to innocent.

Another image that may come to mind is change from having a relationship with God that is crooked to a relationship that is straight. On my computer is a command in the word processor called "justify." It puts the right-hand margin in a straight line.

When we are rescued from the dilemma of sin, this rescue changes our relationship with God from crooked to straight. It changes our status from being guilty before God to being righteous before God.

A second important word is "redemption." "Redemption" has the connotation of liberation, particularly liberation from slavery. The Jewish readers of this letter would have thought about the liberation of Israel from Egypt, or perhaps the story of Hosea buying his wife out of slavery. The Gentile readers' minds would have pictured the slave market where human beings were bought and sold. The image may be of a slave standing on the auction block and being sold to someone. After the sale, the new owner would set the slave free from slavery. The slave's freedom was bought with a price.

Faith . . . is placing your life in God's hands and trusting God to get you to the right destination.

This image reminds us that Jesus Christ paid the price to buy us back from our slavery to sin. Sin had an unbreakable hold on us, but Jesus rescued us by paying the price to set us free.

A third important word in 3:24–25 is translated in the NIV as "sacrifice of atonement" (also in the New Revised Standard Version). Literally the Greek word means *a cover or lid*. It is the word used in the Greek Old Testament for the lid that covered the ark of the covenant. This lid was also known as the mercy seat. The ark with the accompanying lid was housed in the holy of holies in the Jerusalem temple. The ark was understood to be the location of God's presence. Once a year on the Day of Atonement the high priest would enter the holy of holies where the ark was located and make a sacrifice on behalf of the people in order to atone for their sins.

> *We are saved because God has revealed that he will freely rescue us when we accept his gift of grace through faith.*

Jesus Christ is the new *mercy seat*, referring to the location where sins can be forgiven. In the Old Testament the mercy seat was hidden from view, but now God has revealed the mercy seat in the person of Jesus Christ. Jesus is now the place of atonement.

This image helps us understand what being rescued from sin means. All people are rescued from the dilemma of sin in the same way. This rescue occurs because God chose to save people who have faith in Christ.

God's Patience Precedes Punishment (3:25b–26)

Some of the first readers of Paul's Letter to the Romans might have wondered why God had waited so long for exacting wrath on us. Why didn't

Hosea and Redemption

Hosea was an Old Testament prophet whose life story is a testimony to the concept of redemption. Hosea was married to a woman who was perpetually unfaithful as a wife. Her actions led to calamity, and she was finally sold into slavery. By any means of justice, she got what she deserved. Hosea would not have been expected to restore their marital relationship. However, Hosea's love for her motivated him to take all he had and go to the slave auction to buy her back. He brought her back to his home and lived with her as her husband.

Hosea's action illustrated God's redemption of sinful Israel, but it also pointed forward to the redemption people can receive when they trust Christ. Even though we are sinners, God bought us back and restored relationship with us.

God immediately condemn and carry out justice on sinners who were so obviously guilty?

The delay of God's wrath is not evidence that sin is not serious or that God is unconcerned about our guilt. Rather, God's delayed vengeance is evidence of God's mercy. God's patience allows time for the salvation of people who need to hear the good news and repent.

Sin had an unbreakable hold on us, but Jesus rescued us by paying the price to set us free.

In the gospel of Jesus Christ, God has demonstrated both grace and mercy. Grace is a gift from God that we do not deserve. Mercy, on the other hand, is the withholding of punishment that we do deserve. God's merciful withholding of wrath shows us that God wants people to have God's grace. God's desire is for all people to be rescued from the predicament of sin, and God has mercifully held back wrath so that people could be rescued.

We Have Nothing to Brag About (3:27–31)

In Romans 2:17 Paul upbraided the Jews who bragged about their relationship to God because they had the law and thought they were righteous. But they had nothing to brag about any more than the Gentiles had anything to brag about.

The gospel of Jesus Christ takes away every reason for boasting and pride about being righteous before God. The fact is, we have done nothing to deserve God's gift of righteousness, and neither have we done anything to hold back God's wrath. God has done it all.

God's patience allows time for the salvation of people who need to hear the good news and repent.

Boasting is a sin common to all people in all places. Paul lived in a particularly boastful culture. But boasting about our accomplishments reflects a pride that is the root of sinfulness. When it comes to righteousness before God, we have nothing to boast about.

Sometimes we are tempted to boast about our righteousness because of our race, nationality, or religious beliefs. This was certainly the case of Jews who boasted that they were superior to Gentiles. But this kind of boasting did not stop in ancient times.

For example, white people have boasted about superiority because of their race, even to the point of enslaving people of color and taking away their humanity. Men have boasted superiority over women by justifying unjust wages and preventing women from carrying out ministry. In America people appear to boast of being more righteous if they belong to a certain political party or Christian denomination. In fact, many of us boast superiority simply because we are Americans!

God's desire is for all people to be rescued from the predicament of sin. . . .

But there is no room for boasting when we realize that righteousness does not come from our own accomplishments or positions. Everyone stands as equals at the foot of the cross. We are all rescued in the same way, whether we are Jew or Gentile, white or black, male or female. There is no difference. We are all rescued by God's grace when we have faith in Jesus Christ.

Implications and Actions

We all find ourselves in the dilemma of sin. There is nothing we ourselves can do about it, and we are under God's wrath. But there is good news. God wants to rescue us.

God has given us an undeserved gift, and God is now waiting patiently for you to receive that gift through faith in Jesus Christ. But God will not wait forever. Someday you will breathe your last breath, and time will run out. If you have never trusted Jesus, you can do so right now and receive God's gift of rescue. You can have a right relationship with God.

Key Terms to Remember

- Justification—a change of status from guilt to innocence
- Redemption—liberation from bondage, which costs a price
- Sacrifice of atonement—literally, the mercy seat on the ark of the covenant; the location where sins can be forgiven, Jesus Christ
- Mercy—the holding back of deserved punishment
- Grace—a gift we do not deserve
- Faith—complete trust in another

Perhaps you have already experienced God's grace by placing your faith in Jesus. Congratulations! But the temptation may remain to boast, forgetting that your righteousness has nothing to do with political parties, denominations, or your family tree. Your only hope was and is in God's grace.

If you have never trusted Jesus, you can do so right now and receive God's gift of rescue.

The appropriate response to rescue is gratitude. As Christians, let's put aside our bragging rights and rejoice with one another that God's grace and mercy provide rescue for all people who have faith in Jesus.

QUESTIONS

1. What would you tell someone who wants to be baptized because the person believes baptism will "wash away their sins"?

2. This text gives us several images to describe our rescue from sin: "justified," "redemption," and *mercy seat* (3:24–25). Can you think of other biblical images that describe rescue from sin?

3. Since we are all sinners and we all must be saved the same way, what are the implications of the gospel when dealing with racism, sexism, or nationalism?

Background

Romans 4

Main Idea

God's dealings with Abraham show us that right relationship with God has always been based on faith, for everyone.

Question to Explore

Why is faith—not religious rituals and obligations—so important?

Study Aim

To summarize Paul's point about Abraham's faith and state implications for my life

Study and Action Emphases

- Affirm the Bible as our authoritative guide for life and ministry
- Share the gospel with all people
- Develop a growing, vibrant faith

LESSON FIVE

Faith Is the Way

Quick Read

Paul used the story of Abraham as an example of how people have always been made righteous by faith and not by ritual or obligation. Righteousness before God has always been reckoned by God's grace through faith.

Ask people whether they think they will go to heaven when they die, and many will answer like this: *I hope so. I have tried to be a good person. I have done many good things in my life. I have tried to be kind to other people and have been involved in many charities.*

Being kind to people and working with charities is a fine lifestyle, of course. But as we saw in previous lessons, good works is not enough. We are in such a predicament because of sin that the only hope we have is that "righteousness from God comes through faith in Jesus Christ to all who believe" (Romans 3:22a).

In Romans 4 Paul gave an example of what he was talking about. He reached back to a story in the Old Testament to illustrate his point. Abraham was known as the father of the faithful. He was the paragon of virtue, and it was thought that if anyone had ever proved that being a good person could make you right with God, it was Abraham. But Paul used the story of Abraham to illustrate that even Abraham was saved by faith, not works.

Romans 4:1–17, 23–25

[1]What then shall we say that Abraham, our forefather, discovered in this matter? [2]If, in fact, Abraham was justified by works, he had something to boast about—but not before God. [3]What does the Scripture say? "Abraham believed God, and it was credited to him as righteousness."

[4]Now when a man works, his wages are not credited to him as a gift, but as an obligation. [5]However, to the man who does not work but trusts God who justifies the wicked, his faith is credited as righteousness. [6]David says the same thing when he speaks of the blessedness of the man to whom God credits righteousness apart from works:

[7]"Blessed are they
whose transgressions are forgiven,
whose sins are covered.
[8]Blessed is the man
whose sin the Lord will never count against him."

[9]Is this blessedness only for the circumcised, or also for the uncircumcised? We have been saying that Abraham's faith was credited to him as righteousness. [10]Under what circumstances was it credited? Was it after he was circumcised, or before? It was not after, but before! [11]And he received the sign of circumcision, a seal of the righteousness that he had by faith while he was still uncircumcised. So then, he is the father of all

who believe but have not been circumcised, in order that righteousness might be credited to them. **12**And he is also the father of the circumcised who not only are circumcised but who also walk in the footsteps of the faith that our father Abraham had before he was circumcised.

13It was not through law that Abraham and his offspring received the promise that he would be heir of the world, but through the righteousness that comes by faith. **14**For if those who live by law are heirs, faith has no value and the promise is worthless, **15**because law brings wrath. And where there is no law there is no transgression.

16Therefore, the promise comes by faith, so that it may be by grace and may be guaranteed to all Abraham's offspring—not only to those who are of the law but also to those who are of the faith of Abraham. He is the father of us all. **17**As it is written: "I have made you a father of many nations." He is our father in the sight of God, in whom he believed—the God who gives life to the dead and calls things that are not as though they were.

· ·

23The words "it was credited to him" were written not for him alone, **24**but also for us, to whom God will credit righteousness—for us who believe in him who raised Jesus our Lord from the dead. **25**He was delivered over to death for our sins and was raised to life for our justification.

God Is Not in Our Debt (4:1–8)

Paul began his illustration of Abraham with a common rhetorical device called *diatribe*. In diatribe a question is asked as if being asked by another person. Then the question is answered by the writer. Paul often used this device when he anticipated questions that his readers might raise.

Abraham had traditionally been held up as the model of righteousness by works. This view was certainly understandable because Abraham was indeed a good man. He was gracious enough to allow his nephew Lot to have the better land for grazing (Genesis 13). He was a practicing tither, as was revealed when he encountered the priest Melchizedek (Gen. 14). Most notably he was ready to sacrifice his son Isaac (Gen. 22). This event was regarded as a work that was rewarded by God's favor. So Abraham indeed was a good man, and his reputation had followed him down through the annals of time. So it was no wonder that Abraham had long been held up as the model of righteousness by works.

But Paul quoted Genesis 15:6 and put a giant hole in the argument that Abraham was saved by works. "Abraham believed God, and it was credited to him as righteousness" (Rom. 4:3). So even Abraham received God's righteousness by faith!

The word "credited" is an accounting term that means *to add an asset to the ledger sheet.* The King James Version renders the word "reckoned."

> Forgiveness of sin is a blessed gift of God, not something we earn by good works.

Paul's point was that even with all of the good things Abraham did, it was not his good works that were credited to his account. The only thing credited to Abraham's account of righteousness was his faith. Therefore, the man who had traditionally been understood as the prime example of someone who earned righteousness by works was really the prime example of someone who received righteousness by faith!

Paul illustrated this truth from the world of economics. He said that when you work for someone, your pay is something that is owed to you. Your work has put your employer under obligation to pay wages.

But we cannot make God obliged to us. God does not owe us anything. If we could get God's righteousness as a reward for working for him, then we would be controlling God and claiming that we had the power to put God in our debt. It is a common attitude. We think of our relationship to God as a business transaction. If we do something for God, then God is obliged to do something for us. This is the attitude of people who believe they will go to heaven because of what they have done. The logic is that God owes them salvation because of their good works.

Martin Luther Comments

The great reformer Martin Luther (1483–1546) came to understand that righteousness comes only by God's grace through faith in Jesus Christ. He had grown up in a church that had forgotten this truth and claimed that God's grace could be bought from the church. When Luther read Romans, he realized that God could not be bought or sold with money, good works, or religious ritual. In his "Preface to Romans" he wrote: "We reach the conclusion that faith alone justifies us and fulfills the Law; and this because faith brings us the Spirit gained by the merits of Christ. The Spirit, in turn, give us the happiness and freedom at which the Law aims; and this shows that good works really proceed from faith."[1]

The righteousness of God comes only by God's grace, which is received by faith. Righteousness is a gift, not something earned by being a good person. Therefore, Abraham was not saved by good works but by God's grace through faith.

> *The righteousness of God comes only by God's grace, which is received by faith.*

In verses 7–8 Paul backed up this claim again with an Old Testament Scripture. He quoted Psalm 32:1–2, noting that God forgives sin and that the person whose sins are not counted against him is blessed by God. Forgiveness of sin is a blessed gift of God, not something we earn by good works.

Ritual Does Not Result in Righteousness (4:9–12)

Paul then turned to the subject of circumcision. Once again he used the device of diatribe, imagining a questioner asking whether righteousness was reserved for circumcised Jews only.

In Paul's day the Jewish people thought that being a circumcised Jew was enough to be right with God. Since the time of Abraham, circumcision had been a sign of a special covenant with God. The Jewish descendants of Abraham had practiced this ritual throughout the ages. Therefore, this ritual became a sign of who your ancestors were, and particularly a sign that one was a descendant of Abraham, the father of the faithful. The Jewish descendants of Abraham relied on the covenant God had made with Abraham, and they considered circumcision to be a sure sign someone was a part of that covenant.

> *Baptism does not result in righteousness, but rather it is a sign that we have already received God's righteousness by faith.*

Paul pointed out, though, that Abraham had received righteousness before he was circumcised! When we read the story of Abraham in Genesis, we note that Abraham was credited with righteousness in chapter 15 (Gen. 15:6) but was not circumcised until chapter 17. Therefore, Abraham received righteousness while he was technically a Gentile. His circumcision in Genesis 17 was simply a sign that he had already received God's favor.

While not an exact correlation, baptism is a similar sign. As Baptists we believe in believer's baptism. Baptism does not result in righteousness, but rather it is a sign that we have already received God's righteousness by faith.

Since Abraham received righteousness when he was technically a Gentile, Abraham was not only the father of the Jews, but he was also the father of all who receive righteousness by faith whether they are Jews or Gentiles (Rom. 4:11–12)! The Jews thought that for a Gentile to be right with God the Gentile had to be circumcised and become a Jew. In contrast though, Paul made the outrageous claim that in order to be right with God, Jews had to be saved like Gentiles! Once again, the example of Abraham demonstrates that righteousness before God comes by faith alone and not by something we have done to deserve it.

> . . . Righteousness before God comes by faith alone and not by something we have done to deserve it.

Legalism Doesn't Help (4:13–15)

Some might have argued with Paul by claiming that obedience to the law of Moses was what made a person righteous. But Paul reminded his readers that the law of Moses had nothing to do with Abraham's righteousness.

Abraham received his promise of righteousness from God long before Moses was even born. In fact the law did not even come into existence until 400 years after Abraham lived! So Abraham's obedience to the law could not have been what God credited as righteousness to Abraham.

God's promises to Abraham were not on account of the law but on account of faith. So it is with all of Abraham's descendants whether they are Jews or Gentiles. The promises of God are based on faith.

Note that this means that Abraham's descendants are not limited to his natural offspring, to those who can trace their family tree back to him. Abraham's descendants are spiritual children, those who have entered God's family the same way Abraham did, by faith (4:16).

Case Study

Suppose you were talking to a person about the person's relationship to the Lord and he or she said to you, *I think I will go to heaven because I have been a good person. I've always treated people well and given money to charity.* What would you say to the person?

We may be tempted to think that if we carefully follow all the rules, then we will be righteous. We may think that since we have never broken the Ten Commandments we are right with God.

But keeping the Ten Commandments was not the way Abraham received righteousness. Abraham received righteousness simply because he believed God. He had trust in God that led to obedience to God. It was faith and faith alone that allowed him to receive God's promise.

Faith and Faith Alone (4:16–17)

Paul reiterated that it was not good works, circumcision, or the law that made Abraham righteous. It was faith. Faith is the way people are able to receive the grace of God. This was true for Abraham, and it is true for everyone else as well, both Jew and Gentile.

Sometimes people ask me how people who lived in Old Testament times were saved since they did not yet have the revelation of God in Jesus Christ. Admittedly, Jesus had not yet been crucified or resurrected. But Paul made it abundantly clear. People in the Old Testament were saved the same way we are saved: by faith! God's grace was available through faith to people in the Old Testament just as it is today. We are at a great advantage because we are able to look back and see what God has done to demonstrate his grace in Jesus. The people in the Old Testament had to look forward, knowing that they could trust God to do something in the future. But they were saved by trusting God, just as we are.

No matter how good you are and no matter how well you follow the rules, God does not owe you anything.

Abraham, then, was a great example of someone who lived by faith in God. That faith prompted him to live a good life and to submit to circumcision, but faith came first. It was faith that God credited to him as righteousness.

Faith Against All Hope (4:18–22)

Paul recalled another event in the life of Abraham that illustrated his point. When Abraham was past seventy-five years old, God promised that Abraham's descendants would be a great nation and even, as Paul said, be the father of many nations (Gen. 15:5). It was an unlikely promise, to say the least. Yet the Bible tells us that Abraham believed God.

The years progressed, but still no children came. As laughable as it seemed, when Abraham was 100 years old and "Sarah was past the age of childbearing," along came Isaac (Gen. 18:11)! The name Isaac means *laughter,* signifying the great joy they must have had to see God's unlikely promise come to fruition.

> We can do nothing to put God in our debt.

Romans 4:21 gives us a wonderful description of Abraham's faith, affirming that Abraham was "fully persuaded that God had power to do what he had promised." Abraham did not waver in his faith that God would fulfill his promise. That unwavering faith was "credited to him as righteousness" (Rom. 3:22).

Good News for the Rest of Us (4:23–25)

Righteousness by grace through faith was good news to Abraham. But it is good news to us as well. God credits our ledger sheet with righteousness when we, like Abraham, believe God. We even have an advantage over Abraham because we can look back and see what God has already done in Jesus Christ.

> God . . . has promised his righteousness to all who believe in Jesus Christ.

We have a tangible Person to trust—Jesus. We do not need to look into an unknown future and trust God to do something one of these days that will demonstrate God's promises. When we look at Jesus, we see the promise fulfilled when God raised Jesus from the dead. We can see that Jesus died for our sins and was raised by the power of God so that we could be righteous before God.

Implications and Actions

"Abraham believed God and it was credited to him as righteousness" (4:3b). That is how righteousness is credited to us as well: by faith alone.

Maybe you or someone you know has a similar attitude as the common view cited in the first paragraph of this lesson. Maybe you have the attitude that you have been a good person and helped people when you could and that because of your life you are righteous before God. The example of Abraham should make us rethink that kind of attitude.

No matter how good you are and no matter how well you follow the rules, God does not owe you anything. We can do nothing to put God in our debt.

But God has promised to give us a gift we do not deserve. He has promised his righteousness to all who believe in Jesus Christ. Faith and faith alone delivers God's promise of grace.

QUESTIONS

1. Why do so many people believe that being a good person is what it takes to be righteous when the Bible so clearly teaches otherwise?

2. How would you define faith? Can you think of examples either from people you know or people in the Bible that would be good examples of people who have faith?

3. Read Hebrews 11:1. How does this biblical definition of faith compare with the description of Abraham's faith in Romans 4:22?

4. Who are Abraham's offspring?

NOTES

1. Martin Luther, "Preface to Romans," in *Martin Luther: Selections from His Writings,* ed. John Dillenberger (New York: Anchor Books, 1961), 22.

Offering the Best Possible Life

What is God up to? In addition to providing us the way out from a dead-end life (unit one), God is offering us the best possible life (unit two).

"Offering the Best Possible Life" is a four-lesson unit that considers Romans 5—8. These chapters include some of the best known and most loved passages in the Bible. They reveal the Apostle's convictions concerning the freedom that salvation provides and the benefits and blessings that come from the new life in Christ. The lessons in the unit emphasize the benefits of the solution God provides.

Lesson six ("It's a Wonderful Life," Romans 5:1–11) considers the meaning of justification (being declared right in God's sight) by faith and how justification makes living the new life possible. Lesson seven ("It's a New Way of Life," Rom. 6:1–19) challenges believers to live under the Lordship of Christ. Lesson eight ("It's God's Life in You," 8:1–11) calls us to recognize that real life comes by neither surrendering to sinful ways nor trying to keep the rules. This kind of life comes only by allowing the Holy Spirit to dwell in and control us. Lesson nine ("It's a Victorious Life," 8:12–39) offers assurance that God's love will always provide for our needs, even in the most difficult times of our lives.[1]

UNIT TWO. OFFERING THE BEST POSSIBLE LIFE

NOTES

1. Unless otherwise indicated, all Scripture quotations in unit two, lessons six through nine, are from the New International Version.

Focal Text

Romans 5:1–11

Background

Romans 5

Main Idea

Because of what God has done in Christ to offer us justification by faith, we can live a truly wonderful life.

Question to Explore

What sort of life does faith in Christ provide?

Study Aim

To identify benefits of trusting in Christ and consider how I have experienced these blessings

Study and Action Emphases

- Affirm the Bible as our authoritative guide for life and ministry
- Share the gospel with all people
- Develop a growing, vibrant faith

LESSON SIX

It's a Wonderful Life

Quick Read

God through Christ provides believers a wonderful life filled with peace, assurance in adversity, and the realization of the enormity of God's love.

As a boy I went to the barbershop every time my mother forced me! An older man worked there shining shoes. When there were no shoes to be shined, this godly man read his Bible.

He had an interesting habit. If someone simply paid him for the shine, he would say, "Thank you, sir." To those who gave a decent tip, he would say, "Thank *you*, sir." Upon receiving a really good tip, he would exclaim, *"Thank You, Sir!"* The expression in his voice immediately revealed the generous and the stingy. Men gave to receive the expression of appreciation and to be characterized as generous.

One day a man teased the shoeshine man about being a Christian. He asked, *Should a Christian charge twenty-five cents for a shoeshine?* (Remember, this was a long time ago!) The man continued to tease until he finally walked out, to the relief of the shoeshine man and all others in the shop.

The barber apologized to the shoeshine man, saying, "He shouldn't have said those things to you."

The shoeshine man answered, "It doesn't matter. You know, I believe the Bible is true. But I look at it like this, even if it isn't true, it's still a good thing to live by."

In sixty-five years I have never forgotten that teaching. This noble Christian man taught me that the Christian life is a wonderful life, "a good thing to live by"!

We consider in this lesson how wonderful the Christian life really is. In salvation God assures us of a place in heaven. God also assures us of the highest quality of life before eternity. These two great assurances are based on God declaring us right (justifying us) by faith in the death and resurrection of Jesus Christ. God provides for both eternity and the present. The Bible is true, and it is also a good thing to live by! Consider the blessings we have because of all that God has done for us in Christ.

Romans 5:1–11

[1]Therefore, since we have been justified through faith, we have peace with God through our Lord Jesus Christ, [2]through whom we have gained access by faith into this grace in which we now stand. And we rejoice in the hope of the glory of God. [3]Not only so, but we also rejoice in our sufferings, because we know that suffering produces perseverance; [4]perseverance, character; and character, hope. [5]And hope does not

disappoint us, because God has poured out his love into our hearts by the Holy Spirit, whom he has given us.

6You see, at just the right time, when we were still powerless, Christ died for the ungodly. **7**Very rarely will anyone die for a righteous man, though for a good man someone might possibly dare to die. **8**But God demonstrates his own love for us in this: While we were still sinners, Christ died for us.

9Since we have now been justified by his blood, how much more shall we be saved from God's wrath through him! **10**For if, when we were God's enemies, we were reconciled to him through the death of his Son, how much more, having been reconciled, shall we be saved through his life! **11**Not only is this so, but we also rejoice in God through our Lord Jesus Christ, through whom we have now received reconciliation.

Peace with God (5:1–2)

Paul often used the word translated "therefore" to indicate that what he was going to say was based on what he had just said. In this passage, the Apostle indicated that the peace Christians have in salvation is based solidly on what God has done in Christ. Throughout the first four chapters of Romans, Paul had established that all people, Jew and Gentile, were under the condemnation of sin and were separated from God. This separation was of such nature that no human could overcome it.

This noble Christian man taught me that the Christian life is a wonderful life, "a good thing to live by"!

Unsaved people live in a state of separation from God. They may well consider God their enemy. They have no peace but only apprehension and concern. They know only the effects of an alarmed, fearful, and troubled conscience. They should tremble when they think of God's law that they have broken. They should fear God's judgments and cringe at the thought of eternal punishment in hell.

In another letter, the Apostle described the unsaved condition by teaching that before salvation all were dead in transgressions and sins. They were in bondage to the world and Satan, living only to fulfill the desires of the sinful nature. They were the objects of God's wrath (Ephesians 2:2–3). Unsaved people are separated from Christ, excluded from citizenship in God's family, strangers to the promises, "without hope and without God in the world" (Eph. 2:12). They have no assurance of life in eternity or of God's care in the present. They cannot rest on the beautiful truth that God makes good come out of even the worst of their experiences (Romans 8:28).

In Romans 1—4, Paul taught that although all have sinned and all people, Jews and Gentiles, are without peace or hope, God has made a way. God dealt with Abraham in forgiving him of his sin and declaring him justified, that is, in right standing with God. The Lord will give this blessing to us as well.

With Christ, we realize God works for our good even in the midst of afflictions.

God wishes to restore sinful humans to his favor and give the peace that no unsaved person can know. Being "justified" by God's grace, the saved person can know that God has declared him or her in right standing with God. One who trusts in Christ stands acquitted, forgiven, and cleansed. The peace that eludes the one outside of God's family floods in upon the follower of God.

In the experience of being declared right with God, Christians can be at peace. They know that the obstacles on the part of God to reconciliation, arising from God's justice and law, have been removed. God's nature means that God could not just overlook sin and remain consistent with his nature. In the cross God dealt with the problem of sin. In the believer's life, the obstacles arising from sin, rebellion, and conscious guilt are taken away. The path for bringing Holy God and sinful humanity together has been completed.

The outcome of God's plan of salvation produces peace in the believer's mind, a peace the world cannot give and the world cannot take away (Philippians 4:7; 1 Peter 1:8; John 14:27; 16:22). This peace or tranquility is often the first evidence of salvation's transformation. The unbeliever's agitation and troubled heart are replaced by peace and calmness. The unbeliever who considered God as the enemy is now at peace with God and with the entire world.

Faith in God provides a wonderful life in both good times and trying times.

This state of peace comes "through our Lord Jesus Christ" (Rom. 5:1). God gives this peace by means of the believer's experience with the Lord Jesus. There is no other way!

Paul continued to speak of the peace one receives in Christ, saying that believers have an "access"—entrance or introduction—into the very "glory" of God through faith in Christ. Believers "now stand" in this state of grace and confidently and joyfully look forward to participating in the glory of God (5:2). The word "hope"

> *Christ died in our place when we were still mired in our sin and rebellion.*

should be understood as *confidence* or *assurance*. "Glory" refers to *participation in the greatness and perfection of God.*

Indeed, what a wonderful life!

Security in Life (5:3–5)

Paul not only stressed the peace that one has in salvation but also moved forward to show another aspect of the wonderful life God provides. Believers have a deep and abiding sense of peace, and they also can "rejoice" (perhaps better, *exult*) even in trials that may come their way.

Words About the Christian Life

Justified

>   **Meaning**: declared in right standing with God
>   **Time of occurrence**: instantaneous at salvation, once and for all
>   **Source**: trusting in Christ for salvation

Sanctified

>   **Meaning**: guided to become progressively what God has already declared the believer to be
>   **Time of occurrence**: an ungoing process throughout the believer's life
>   **Source**: the action of the Holy Spirit within a believer

Glorified

>   **Meaning**: the blessing of being in the presence of God
>   **Time of occurrence**: a process that begins at salvation, continues in the Christian life, and becomes full in eternity with God
>   **Source**: made certain by faith in Christ's resurrection

Christians can rejoice in times of prosperity and health. Paul also showed that God's wonderful life is beneficial in producing support in trials. The word "sufferings" refers to all kinds of trials that Christians are called to endure. Christians' assurance of well-being lasts through afflictions because we "know" that in the afflictions God will work or produce a miracle of "perseverance." Perhaps a helpful synonym for "perseverance" is *patience*. *Patience* is that calm temper that suffers evils without murmuring or discontent. The Scriptures speak often of this blessing of care in trials (Matthew 5:11–12; James 1:2–3, 12; 1 Pet. 4:12–14).

We should accept God's offer of justification and rejoice in the peace God provides.

Without Christ, we are irritated and troubled by trials. Without Christ, we complain and become more and more obstinate and rebellious because we have no source of consolation or strength. Without Christ, we can let trials drive us away from God.

With Christ, on the other hand, we realize the Father's hand of care even in the trials. We place our faith in God's wisdom and goodness. With Christ, we realize God works for our good even in the midst of afflictions.

For Christians, God's support during trials produces "perseverance" or *patience*. Often those Christians who are the most severely afflicted are the most patient.

Patient endurance, says the Apostle, produces "character." The word referred to a thorough examination by which the quality or nature of a thing was ascertained. By such an examination, something would be tested and approved. As used here, the term refers to God's approval, with the meaning that when "suffering produces perseverance," then "perseverance" produces God's approval.

This wonderful life God provides can help us through all trials.

Afflictions, borne patiently, show how strong we are. The trials test our faith and prove it genuine.

"Character," then, produces "hope." "Hope" is *assurance*. Living through adversity shows that one's faith is genuine and results in "hope," sustaining the soul. This "hope" never lets the believer down. It never disappoints. This "hope" or assurance stands firm because God has poured out his love into our hearts by the work of the Holy Spirit and will continue to do so.

The Apostle beautifully described the various steps and stages of the benefits God provides in a manner well attested by the experiences of God's children. Faith in God provides a wonderful life in both good times and trying times.

Knowledge of God's Love (5:6–11)

The wonderful blessings of God's justification of believers continue in their ongoing knowledge of God's love and provision. At just the right time, when humankind was weak or powerless to overcome Satan and sin, God gave Christ to die for the ungodly. God's great gift came in response to our immense need.

Paul compared the enormity of this expression of love in Christ Jesus to the far inferior expressions of concern by humans. The Apostle declared that for a very good person ("righteous man") some might be willing to die. But God's undeserved love was directed to humankind while we were "still sinners" (Rom. 5:8). Christ died in our place when we were still mired in our sin and rebellion.

As believers who experience the wonder of salvation, let us share this good news with all people.

The knowledge of the depth of this love astounds all who experience it. Believers are declared right with God because of the death of Jesus on the cross. Even while we were God's enemies, God offered reconciliation to us, calling us back to himself through Jesus. The life, death, and resurrection of Jesus provide the wonderful life of Christians.

Applying These Truths

Few passages are so filled with life-changing truth. Although ever aware of our sinful and helpless condition, we have received from the Father a promise of eternal life, which gives peace, the assurance of care in trials, and the realization of the enormity of God's gift. We should accept God's offer of justification and rejoice in the peace God provides.

This wonderful life God provides can help us through all trials. We can exult in afflictions because we know that God will use these experiences to produce in us perseverance, prove the genuineness of our faith, and show us how great his love for us really is.

May we trust in God's justifying grace, live in his assuring care amid trials, and rejoice in the knowledge of God's great love as revealed in the provision of his Son. As believers who experience the wonder of salvation, let us share this good news with all people.

QUESTIONS

1. How does God's provision of salvation affect our sense of guilt?

2. Do you ever think when trials come upon you that God is punishing you? What do the truths in this lesson teach us about suffering?

3. How does the experience of walking through adversity with God prove the genuineness of the believer's faith?

4. In what ways do you experience peace with God?

5. Do you sometimes hold back from sharing your experience of new life in Christ with others? Why?

Focal Text

Romans 6:1–19

Background

Romans 5:12—6:23

Main Idea

When we enter into relationship with God by faith in Christ, we are to walk in newness of life and to live under Christ's Lordship.

Question to Explore

What difference does being a Christian make in how you live?

Study Aim

To state why being baptized into Christ and thus being under his Lordship should make a difference in my life and to identify implications for my life

Study and Action Emphases

- Affirm the Bible as our authoritative guide for life and ministry
- Share the gospel with all people
- Develop a growing, vibrant faith

LESSON SEVEN

It's a New Way of Life

Quick Read

In Christ, God has declared us right with him because he has forgiven our sin. We should, therefore, allow the Spirit to guide us to live a new life.

In her classic novel *To Kill a Mockingbird*, Harper Lee described the scene at the first day of school for Scout, lawyer Atticus Finch's young daughter. When the teacher discovered that Scout's schoolmate, Walter Cunningham, had no lunch, she tried to give him lunch money. The boy looked at the money and then handed it back, saying, "No ma'am, I don't think."

The exasperated teacher could not understand the boy's refusal. Scout tried to explain, "Ma'am, he's a Cunningham." The local people understood. Cunninghams never accepted any help and never borrowed any money. Something about being a Cunningham assured a certain response.[1]

In a far more significant way, being a Christian should assure certain responses. The relationship of being a Christian should motivate a person to live in a Christian way. Christians should do certain things and not do other things. The Bible explains the kind of life Christians should practice.

This lesson considers the difference being a Christian makes in a person's behavior. The Scriptures teach us that when believers by faith in Christ enter a new relationship with God, they should begin to practice a new way of life.

Romans 6:1–19

[1]What shall we say, then? Shall we go on sinning so that grace may increase? [2]By no means! We died to sin; how can we live in it any longer? [3]Or don't you know that all of us who were baptized into Christ Jesus were baptized into his death? [4]We were therefore buried with him through baptism into death in order that, just as Christ was raised from the dead through the glory of the Father, we too may live a new life.

[5]If we have been united with him like this in his death, we will certainly also be united with him in his resurrection. [6]For we know that our old self was crucified with him so that the body of sin might be done away with, that we should no longer be slaves to sin—[7]because anyone who has died has been freed from sin.

[8]Now if we died with Christ, we believe that we will also live with him. [9]For we know that since Christ was raised from the dead, he cannot die again; death no longer has mastery over him. [10]The death he died, he died to sin once for all; but the life he lives, he lives to God. [11]In the same way, count yourselves dead to sin but alive to God in

Christ Jesus. **12**Therefore do not let sin reign in your mortal body so that you obey its evil desires. **13**Do not offer the parts of your body to sin, as instruments of wickedness, but rather offer yourselves to God, as those who have been brought from death to life; and offer the parts of your body to him as instruments of righteousness. **14**For sin shall not be your master, because you are not under law, but under grace.

15What then? Shall we sin because we are not under law but under grace? By no means! **16**Don't you know that when you offer yourselves to someone to obey him as slaves, you are slaves to the one whom you obey—whether you are slaves to sin, which leads to death, or to obedience, which leads to righteousness? **17**But thanks be to God that, though you used to be slaves to sin, you wholeheartedly obeyed the form of teaching to which you were entrusted. **18**You have been set free from sin and have become slaves to righteousness.

19I put this in human terms because you are weak in your natural selves. Just as you used to offer the parts of your body in slavery to impurity and to ever-increasing wickedness, so now offer them in slavery to righteousness leading to holiness.

Free, Free, at Last (6:1–4)

In Jakarta, Indonesia, a beautiful statue pictures Indonesia's independence from Holland. The work shows an Indonesian man holding over his head his manacled wrists. The chains that had bound his arms, however, are shown as broken. The statue is appropriately named, "Merkeka," which in the language of Indonesia means *freedom.*

Freedom is important to every person in every country. In the Christian life, freedom has even more significance. The salvation that God gives in Christ frees the believer from the power and bondage of sin. The believer can say with great faith and gratitude, *I am free, free at last, from dominion by sin and Satan.*

Romans 6:1 logically follows Romans 5:18–21. The Apostle had taught that sin, death, and bondage entered human experience by the sin of one person, Adam. But life and freedom from sin had come in Christ and freed from the power of sin and evil all people who would accept God's offer. Believers thus are "justified," or *declared right with God and free from the guilt of sin.* The Holy Spirit brings to the Christian what the Bible calls sanctification, that is, the process of changing us and developing us into that which God has already declared us to be (see chart in lesson six).

In Romans 6:2, Paul answered the question asked in verse 1. Perhaps some were asking that question, or Paul may have merely used the question rhetorically. *Shall we continue to sin so that God might continue to demonstrate and provide his wonderful forgiving grace?*

Paul answered in the most forceful way possible in the Greek language, *May it never be! How,* he asked, *could one who has died to sin possibly choose to remain in its clutches?* To be dead to anything is a strong expression indicating that the person has no further relationship with the matter and that the thing has no more influence on the person. One who is dead is unaffected by the situations of this life and is not attracted to cries for pleasure and ambition. Christians have died to sin. So sin has lost its influence over them, and they are not subject to it (see Galatians 2:19; Colossians 3:3; 1 Peter 2:24).

The Bible explains the kind of life Christians should practice.

Even though Christians have died to sin, they are not dead to sin in this life. In other words, believers die to sin in Christ Jesus, but they are not totally separated from enticements to evil. We do reach the state where we desire to live for God rather than for sin, but we do not totally escape the temptations to wrong. The Apostle asked, in effect, *How can we who have recognized the evil of sin and by solemn promise have rejected it continue to practice it?* Sin becomes abhorrent to the very nature of the Christian.

Immersion in water is the biblical model for baptism and most adequately expresses the fullest meaning of the act.

Romans 6:3–4 refers to baptism, but the meaning is not limited to literal water baptism. Even so, we must not overlook or minimize the importance of baptism in water by immersion. Immersion in water is the biblical model for baptism and most adequately expresses the fullest meaning of the act. In the act of being immersed in water on profession of faith in Christ, a believer portrays the fact of his or her turning to God in Christ.

The emphasis of these verses, though, is that in baptism we are identified with the death of Christ and will therefore be identified with his life (see also 1 Corinthians 12:13). Through the full meaning of baptism, Christians are joined to the living Christ and should, therefore, "live a new life" (Rom. 6:4). To "live a new life" supposes newness of heart. The Greek word translated "live" carries the idea of walking. Thus the thought is that believers walk by new rules, toward new goals, and by new principles.

To Kill a Mockingbird

The novel *To Kill a Mockingbird* by Harper Lee won the Pulitzer Prize and was made into a movie. The book tells the story of racial mistreatment and injustice in the days of segregation. The book's title comes from the thought that such behavior was like "killing a mockingbird," a wrong against beauty and goodness that should not be done. In a sense, the book called for a new way of life by confronting racial injustice.

In our own day, are any mockingbirds in danger? What should Christians do?

Living in Jesus (6:5–10)

Paul pointed out in verse 5 that believers have been "united" in identification with Christ's death. He declared that Christians shall also be "united" with Christ in the likeness of his resurrection.

The word often translated "united" can carry the image of being *planted*. The image may be of plants growing one upon the other as mistletoe grows on the oak, deriving nourishment from it. The image of being planted could also refer to the process of grafting, whereby one plant is grafted onto another. In yet another understanding, the Apostle could have been calling to mind the image of a seed that is planted in the ground, drawing its nourishment and strength from the

In the act of being immersed in water on profession of faith in Christ, a believer portrays the fact of his or her turning to God in Christ.

earth and thereby growing, developing, and producing fruit. Whichever variation of the meaning of the image is chosen, the meaning intended may be that the death and resurrection of Jesus Christ is the cause and source of all Christian fruitfulness. Paul was teaching that believers are *planted* in Christ's death and resurrection and live and serve by Christ's power. So Christians derive their growth, strength, and fruitfulness from Christ's death and resurrection. From Christ stems not only the motivation but also the empowerment for following the Christian life. This new life comes from the new relationship with God in Christ.

Paul next pointed to two great realizations that we who believe in Christ "know" (6:6–9). First, believers "know" they are freed from the power of sin, for their old self was "crucified with him" (6:6). The word

In His Steps

The classic book *In His Steps* by Charles M. Sheldon tells of a group of Christians who decided they would take seriously the claims of Christ by asking of every action what Jesus would do. Set in the nineteenth century, the book pictures the changes that occurred in various people's lives as they considered seriously how they should live as Christians. Their taking Jesus seriously meant a new way of life. What if you took Jesus and his teachings more seriously? What would you start doing? What would you stop doing? What would your new way of life be like?

"crucified" shows the drastic nature of the death of Christ and also the totality by which the body of sin is destroyed. Note that this experience is done *for* us. No one can crucify himself or herself. The Spirit must do this in us. Christians thus are freed from sin and empowered to live with Christ.

> *. . . Christians derive their growth, strength, and fruitfulness from Christ's death and resurrection.*

Second, Paul said we "know" that Christ is ever living (6:9). Christ died, but he is alive today. Because of Christ's death and resurrection, he can save all who will turn to him.

Instruments Used by God (6:11–14)

Christians are then to "count" themselves "dead to sin but alive to God" (6:11). Sin should not, therefore, reign in the lives of believers (6:11–12).

Since believers are dead to sin and alive in Christ, they should "offer" themselves to be available as instruments of God's ministry (6:13). The "parts of your body" (6:13) are all the abilities, opportunities, and possibilities you possess. Believers must never allow these abilities and opportunities to be used as instruments or tools of unrighteousness.

Satan strives to use believers to express unkindness, lead others into sin, turn a deaf ear to calls for help, misuse God's creation, or do less than what they know to be the will of God. The "parts of your body," though, are fearfully and wonderfully made and never should be Satan's tools of unrighteousness.

On the other hand, Christians should devote every "part" of themselves to God and to his service. Their tongues should be consecrated to God's praise, to the proclamation of God's truth, and to the expression of God's kindness. Their hands should be active in useful labor for God and God's cause. Their feet should be moving on the pathway of God's service. Their eyes should contemplate God's works to express thanksgiving and praise to him. Their ears should be open to hear the voice of God as God utters his will in Scripture, creation, and history. God speaks to us every day, and we should with joy hear him.

> *God can use us as God's tools to accomplish God's will.*

The "parts" of Christians' bodies are tools for God's use. Tools are important to most work. The results, however, come from the one who uses the tools rather than from the tools themselves. My son, a professional cabinetmaker, can use the same tools I try to use. His product comes out square, strong, and beautiful. My results are crooked, shaky, and inferior.

We often think we do not have the abilities and opportunities to do great things for God. As a matter of fact, what is done through us depends far less on our abilities than it does on the simple act by which we place our abilities and opportunities in God's hands. God can use us as God's tools to accomplish God's will.

> *The new life in Christ frees believers from the power and bondage of sin. . . .*

We can, therefore, present or offer to God our abilities and opportunities, and God will use them to produce the most beautiful and wonderful of products and results. Does this not inspire us? We should never hold back from allowing our lives to be used by God in God's work, knowing that God can produce great things through us when we do.

Freed from Slavery to Sin (6:15–19)

The Apostle declared that believers can live for Christ because they have been freed from slavery to sin. In the old life, unbelievers were slaves to sin, but now God has declared them to be in right standing with him and is making them his followers. Believers have been freed from sin and can serve God in righteousness.

Summary

The new life in Christ frees believers from the power and bondage of sin and makes Christian living possible. Because believers are "united with" or *planted in* Christ (6:5), they receive the strength and power from him to live the life God desires. Believers who are free of the power of sin can serve God and others by presenting their bodies (abilities, opportunities, influences) to God in his service.

Applying These Truths

1. Christians can live in the assurance that God has declared them right with him and forgiven their sins.
2. Christians should accept their freedom from sin and live by the power of Christ the lives God has planned for them.
3. Christians should accept the truth that they can live in Christ and serve him by serving others.
4. Christians should realize that Satan will attempt to use them as tools in Satan's efforts to bring harm to the world and to other people.
5. Christians can be certain God will use their lives and abilities as tools in his work if they will allow him to do so.

QUESTIONS

1. Do you have the assurance that you can indeed overcome sin through the new life Christ gives you? Do you find yourself in doubt of your ability to overcome Satan? How can this passage of Scripture help?

2. How would you answer a person who says, *I am under grace not law, and therefore I can live however I want to?*

3. What instances do you recall when you allowed yourself to be used as an instrument of Satan to cause harm or evil to others?

4. How does God want to use you as his instrument in his great work of saving and caring for people in this world?

NOTES

1. Harper Lee, *To Kill a Mockingbird* (New York: J. P. Lippencott, 1960), 25.

Study Aim

To explore why the life of God's Spirit in us provides real life and to identify implications for our lives

Background

Romans 7:1—8:11

Main Idea

The way to real life is through neither surrendering to sin nor keeping the rules but through allowing God's Spirit to dwell within us by faith in Christ.

Study and Action Emphases

- Affirm the Bible as our authoritative guide for life and ministry
- Share the gospel with all people
- Develop a growing, vibrant faith

Question to Explore

What is the way to real life?

LESSON EIGHT

It's God's Life in You

Quick Read

People cannot attain real life or know peace and assurance by either following sinful behavior or attempting to keep biblical (or other) rules rigorously. A life of peace and service is possible when we allow God to draw us into the fellowship of salvation in the Holy Spirit.

Augustine, one of the greatest interpreters of the Christian faith (A.D. 354–430), lived a sinful life, seeking to find his life through sinful behavior, prior to his conversion. God's grace in Christ found Augustine and brought him lovingly to salvation. After his conversion, Augustine wrote in his celebrated book, *The Confessions of St. Augustine,* that before salvation he was in captivity to sin but in redemption, God had set him free and made genuine life possible.[1]

Martin Luther (1483–1546), in a moment of panic during a thunderstorm, cried out, "Save me and I will become a monk." Luther did become a monk and with great determination tried to keep every law and rule of the church. This way of rule keeping, however, did not satisfy. Only when Luther came to realize and accept that God saves only through faith did he find the satisfaction he sought.[2]

These two men sought genuine life—one through sinful living and one through rigorous rule keeping. Both failed to find real life. Only when they came to Jesus and found in him forgiveness from sin and the indwelling empowerment of the Holy Spirit did they find real life.

The Apostle Paul understood this great truth centuries earlier than either Augustine or Luther. Paul wrote in Romans that real life comes neither from surrendering to sinful behavior nor from finding and following more rigorous rules. Real life comes only when we allow the Holy Spirit to live within us and thus experience victory over sin and peace with God through this relationship in Christ.

To find peace and joy in Christ, believers must be freed from the power of sin, which no person can resist, and the tyranny of the law, which no person can fulfill. The life Paul promised is realized only when the Holy Spirit lives within the believer.

Romans 8:1–11

[1]Therefore, there is now no condemnation for those who are in Christ Jesus, [2]because through Christ Jesus the law of the Spirit of life set me free from the law of sin and death. [3]For what the law was powerless to do in that it was weakened by the sinful nature, God did by sending his own Son in the likeness of sinful man to be a sin offering. And so he condemned sin in sinful man, [4]in order that the righteous requirements of the law might be fully met in us, who do not live according to the sinful nature but according to the Spirit.

> ⁵Those who live according to the sinful nature have their minds set on what that nature desires; but those who live in accordance with the Spirit have their minds set on what the Spirit desires. ⁶The mind of sinful man is death, but the mind controlled by the Spirit is life and peace; ⁷the sinful mind is hostile to God. It does not submit to God's law, nor can it do so. ⁸Those controlled by the sinful nature cannot please God.
>
> ⁹You, however, are controlled not by the sinful nature but by the Spirit, if the Spirit of God lives in you. And if anyone does not have the Spirit of Christ, he does not belong to Christ. ¹⁰But if Christ is in you, your body is dead because of sin, yet your spirit is alive because of righteousness. ¹¹And if the Spirit of him who raised Jesus from the dead is living in you, he who raised Christ from the dead will also give life to your mortal bodies through his Spirit, who lives in you.

No Condemnation by God (8:1–4)

Romans 8 is one of the most inspiring, assuring, loved, quoted, and remembered passages in the entire Bible. This wonderful passage begins with "no condemnation" (sentence of wrong or guilt), ends with *no separation* (8:31–39), and in between claims the assurance of eternal life and the conviction that all things work together for good to those who love God (8:9–28).

Paul began this passage with his often-used method of stating "therefore." With this term, he pointed back to what he had already taught, primarily in chapters 6 and 7. Before salvation, people live under the control of Satan and sin and cannot overcome temptations to wrong living. People also live under the oppression of the law (Mosaic law) and the law of the flesh. But God in Christ has set believers free from sin and the law and made possible peace with God and service in God's kingdom.

Romans 7:13–25 has received varying interpretations. Many interpreters are convinced the chapter is autobiographical. According to that view, these words describe Paul's own experience of striving and struggling against evil and finding that in human strength victory was not possible. Two alternatives exist within this viewpoint. Some consider the words to describe Paul's experience before his conversion and others think the descriptions are of his experiences after his saving encounter with Christ.

Still other interpreters think Paul was describing not his own personal experiences but rather that of historical Israel in receiving and being unable to fulfill the Mosaic law. This interpretation notes that the use of the term "I" in the passage was a rhetorical method frequently employed in Jewish literature. The term "I" thus refers to Israel, not to Paul the individual. Again two different approaches are seen in this interpretation. One is that at times Jewish teaching would use "I" to speak in a way that did not include the writer in the experience (see 1 Corinthians 13:1–3). A more likely approach in this interpretation suggests that in Romans 7, the term "I" denotes the people of Israel and their experiences of missing the fullest intent of God's revelations and God's law, with the writer identifying with these experiences. An example of Old Testament usage of the first person pronoun to indicate Israel is Micah 7:8–10. Paul identified with the experiences of Israel as did other Jewish people of his day.

Only when they came to Jesus and found in him forgiveness from sin and the indwelling empowerment of the Holy Spirit did they find real life.

I am inclined to follow the view that Paul was speaking of his own struggle to follow God's will even after his conversion. The interesting fact is, however, that any of the views about Paul's meaning (concerning his own life or that of Israel) in the end leads to very nearly the same understanding.

In Romans 6—7, Paul indicated that people are under the power of sin and Satan and cannot overcome this power in their own strength. He showed that people are also under the power of law and cannot reach the requirements. Paul declared in Romans 7:1–6 that people remain under the power of the law as long as they live. However, as a woman married to a man is free of that relationship on the death of her husband, people who are dead to the law are no longer under the power of the law.

To find peace and joy in Christ, believers must be freed from the power of sin, which no person can resist, and the tyranny of the law, which no person can fulfill.

People who are free from the law are now free to produce good fruit in proper actions toward God.

The Apostle stressed that Christians no longer must seek to serve God through following rules and customs in some mechanical way. They can now serve God with all their hearts and minds. The law of God served to convict of sinfulness, which Paul says he would never have known apart from the revelation of the law. Paul's understanding of the law made him aware of his sinfulness in violating the law.

Paul quickly denied that he meant that the law was bad. It was not the law that was at fault. Rather, Paul's inability to keep the law had plunged him into despair. The law of the flesh—that is, his sinful tendencies—led him into rebellion against God. Sin controlled him. The Apostle spoke in anguish that what he despised was exactly what he did, and what he desired above all else was what he failed to do. Paul was convinced that something deep within him, his old sinful nature, continued enticing him to evil (7:7–14).

Paul cried out with the query, *How shall I escape this sinful state?* (See 7:24.) He could not do it within his own power. He could not claim victory in rigorously keeping the law. With great thanksgiving, the Apostle testified that the victory over sin and law had been accomplished by God through Jesus Christ, who had set him free (7:25).

Only when Luther came to realize and accept that God saves only through faith did he find the satisfaction he sought.

Because God has freed believers from sin and the law, there is therefore now no condemnation for those who belong by faith to Jesus. Paul, in 8:1, placed the "no" first in the sentence in the Greek to emphasize the idea. Not one trace of guilt or weight of wrong faces or frightens believers. "Now" sets the timeline, meaning that this state of "no condemnation" exists after salvation.

Believers are not subject to charges of guilt or to the punishments that accompany guilt (6:2–3). This wonderful freedom from the power of sin and death comes not by human effort but rather by the life-giving power of the Holy Spirit through Jesus Christ. The law could not lift one from

Paul's Use of Flesh and Body

Paul did not use the terms *body* and *flesh* in the sense of merely the biological mechanism that humans use during life. The Greeks considered humans as body (material) and soul (immaterial). The Greek view of the body and soul was thus a strict dualism. The New Testament writers (including Paul), however, followed the Hebrew concept that humans were a unity of body and soul that could not be separated. So when Paul used the term *flesh* he meant not merely a part of a person but the entire human existence. This Hebrew view of a human being as a unity leads Christians to the understanding of the necessity of resurrection of the body and not just the soul.

the bondage of sin, not because of any weakness in the law, but because of the weakness of the human flesh. Human nature rebels against God. God, however, provided the power to escape the bondage of sin by sending Jesus Christ, his Son, "in the likeness of sinful man," that is, in the incarnation of Jesus (8:3). Sin was defeated when Jesus died on the cross as the perfect sacrifice for sin (see Hebrews 4:14–16).

This wonderful freedom from the power of sin and death comes not by human effort but rather by the life-giving power of the Holy Spirit through Jesus Christ.

This new plan God provides for reaching real life does not come through knowing the rules of God. These laws are ineffective because humans cannot keep them. The new plan can lead to real life because God destroyed the power of sin and death through sending his own Son to provide the sacrifice for our sin. The death of Jesus satisfied all the "righteous requirements of the law" (Rom. 8:4). People cannot in their own strength become right with God. God, however, can now declare believers right with him because the sin debt is paid and the sacrifice complete. People can now live in the Spirit rather than according to the sinful nature (8:3–4).

Because believers are freed from the tyranny of sin and law, they can now actually have hope of obeying God's laws and repulsing the claims of the old sinful nature (8:4). The strength of the old nature is intense, and humans cannot win the battle. The law shows the evil and confronts humans with their sinfulness. But God in Christ has opened the new way so believers can turn away from the evil, turn to the light, and find the meaningful life God promises.

. . . God in Christ has set believers free from sin and the law and made possible peace with God and service in God's kingdom.

Living in God's Spirit (8:5–10)

The Christian does not face the struggle with Satan, sin, and law in human strength. The struggle is not that of the believer striving against sin and the old nature. Paul noted in Romans 8:5–6 that rather it is the Holy Spirit striving against sin. Those who live according to the sinful nature seek only what nature drives them to desire. Those who are living by the indwelling Spirit, however, have their entire beings (their mindset) directed to what the Spirit desires. The person committed to the Spirit's directions has life, peace, and the possibility of pleasing God (8:5–8).

The Apostle contrasted the life of one who is living according to the flesh—that is, the sinful nature—and one who is living in the Spirit. Note the contrasts in the traits of the two types of living:

Life in the Flesh	Life in the Spirit of God
Committed to the desires of sinful flesh	Committed to the desires of God
Death	Life and peace
Hostile to God	Controlled by God
Cannot and will not submit to God	Free to obey God
Cannot please God	Can please God
Lives only in fear and terror	Has peace and assurance

Only believers can live in the Spirit of God. One who does not have this indwelling Spirit is not of God. God deals with the sin nature not by trying to repair it but rather by giving a new nature. Paul said, " . . . if Christ is in you [meaning *he certainly is*], your body is dead because of sin, yet your spirit is alive because of righteousness" (8:10). The body no longer controls, but Christ controls. The believer's spirit is alive because of the great righteousness of Christ that bought us back from our sin (8:10).

Assurance in the Holy Spirit (8:11)

The Apostle did not speak with doubt concerning the salvation of the people to whom he was writing. He actually said *since* "the Spirit who raised Jesus from the dead is living in you," then these believers could have assurance that the Spirit would make their dead bodies live again. This teaching assures believers of eternal life with God. Life in the flesh has no such assurance. Life in the Holy Spirit has full assurance.

Applying These Truths

1. Christians should live in the assurance that we have been declared in right standing with God. This assurance includes knowing that the Holy Spirit will bring our bodies to life after physical death.

2. Christians should recognize that while they can never fully keep the law of God, in Christ's life and death God has provided forgiveness of sin and new life in Jesus.
3. Christians should reflect daily on the tremendous grace God demonstrated in Jesus' coming to this earth (the incarnation), sacrificial death (the cross), certain and historical rising from the dead (the resurrection), going back to heaven (the ascension), and promised return (Second Coming).
4. Believers should serve God with confidence, knowing that the Holy Spirit empowers their service.

QUESTIONS

1. What behaviors or attitudes in your life make you sometimes despair of living up to God's expectations of you? What do you do in these times?

2. How do you deal with doubts that may arise in your mind concerning your salvation?

3. Do you sometimes forget or at least lose sight of the truth that in Christ Jesus God has declared you in right standing with him? How can we continue to focus on this truth?

4. Have you ever felt trapped by the idea that you might be unable to fulfill God's will? What is the answer?

NOTES

1. See Augustine, *Confessions*, Book 2, chapters 7, 10; Book 8, chapter 12; Book 9, chapter 1.
2. Roland H. Bainton, *Here I Stand* (Nashville, Tennessee: Abingdon Cokesbury, 1950), 21, 23–51.

Focal Text

Romans 8:12–39

Background

Romans 8:12–39

Main Idea

The Christian life, although not exempt from struggle and suffering, is victorious because of the love of God in Christ Jesus our Lord.

Question to Explore

Where can we find help in the midst of our greatest struggles and sufferings?

Study Aim

To identify teachings in this passage that offer assurance that the Christian life is victorious in spite of the presence of struggle and suffering

Study and Action Emphases

- Affirm the Bible as our authoritative guide for life and ministry
- Share the gospel with all people
- Develop a growing, vibrant faith

LESSON NINE

It's a Victorious Life

Quick Read

As do all people, Christians live in a fallen world and face struggles, trials, and suffering. Christians, however, can face difficulties with assurance because of God's continuing care, Christ's completed work, and the Holy Spirit's personal ministry.

"The thrill of victory and the agony of defeat." You likely have heard those words many times. You may even recall the video introduction to the popular television sports program that used them.[1] In the video, the skier flashes down the slope to the ski jump ramp. Something goes tragically wrong, and the skier begins a head-over-heels fall down the mountain. The announcer then speaks the memorable words, "The thrill of victory and the agony of defeat."

No one watching the video wants to experience "the agony of defeat" in the way the skier did, of course. More important than victory in a sporting event, though, is the victory of which this passage of Scripture, Romans 8:12–39, speaks. Christians crave victory over sin, fear, trials, and, in the final moment, death. The most important truth in this lesson is that these great victories in the Christian life are both certain and possible because of the safety God provides in salvation and the assurance of God's sufficient love in Christ Jesus.

Romans 8:12–39

[12]Therefore, brothers, we have an obligation—but it is not to the sinful nature, to live according to it. [13]For if you live according to the sinful nature, you will die; but if by the Spirit you put to death the misdeeds of the body, you will live, [14]because those who are led by the Spirit of God are sons of God. [15]For you did not receive a spirit that makes you a slave again to fear, but you received the Spirit of sonship. And by him we cry, "*Abba*, Father." [16]The Spirit himself testifies with our spirit that we are God's children. [17]Now if we are children, then we are heirs—heirs of God and co-heirs with Christ, if indeed we share in his sufferings in order that we may also share in his glory.

[18]I consider that our present sufferings are not worth comparing with the glory that will be revealed in us. [19]The creation waits in eager expectation for the sons of God to be revealed. [20]For the creation was subjected to frustration, not by its own choice, but by the will of the one who subjected it, in hope [21]that the creation itself will be liberated from its bondage to decay and brought into the glorious freedom of the children of God.

[22]We know that the whole creation has been groaning as in the pains of childbirth right up to the present time. [23]Not only so, but we ourselves, who have the firstfruits of the Spirit, groan inwardly as we wait eagerly for our adoption as sons, the redemption of our bodies. [24]For in this hope we

were saved. But hope that is seen is no hope at all. Who hopes for what he already has? **²⁵** But if we hope for what we do not yet have, we wait for it patiently.

²⁶ In the same way, the Spirit helps us in our weakness. We do not know what we ought to pray for, but the Spirit himself intercedes for us with groans that words cannot express. **²⁷** And he who searches our hearts knows the mind of the Spirit, because the Spirit intercedes for the saints in accordance with God's will.

²⁸ And we know that in all things God works for the good of those who love him, who have been called according to his purpose. **²⁹** For those God foreknew he also predestined to be conformed to the likeness of his Son, that he might be the firstborn among many brothers. **³⁰** And those he predestined, he also called; those he called, he also justified; those he justified, he also glorified.

³¹ What, then, shall we say in response to this? If God is for us, who can be against us? **³²** He who did not spare his own Son, but gave him up for us all—how will he not also, along with him, graciously give us all things? **³³** Who will bring any charge against those whom God has chosen? It is God who justifies. **³⁴** Who is he that condemns? Christ Jesus, who died— more than that, who was raised to life—is at the right hand of God and is also interceding for us. **³⁵** Who shall separate us from the love of Christ? Shall trouble or hardship or persecution or famine or nakedness or danger or sword? **³⁶** As it is written:

"For your sake we face death all day long;
    we are considered as sheep to be slaughtered."

³⁷ No, in all these things we are more than conquerors through him who loved us. **³⁸** For I am convinced that neither death nor life, neither angels nor demons, neither the present nor the future, nor any powers, **³⁹** neither height nor depth, nor anything else in all creation, will be able to separate us from the love of God that is in Christ Jesus our Lord.

Victory over Sin (8:12–14)

Every believer faces the intense struggle to overcome temptation and sin. The Apostle Paul consistently repeated in the previous chapters of Romans the truth that no person can win this battle against sin in his or her own strength. He expressed these great conclusions:

- "All have sinned and come short of the glory of God" (Romans 3:23; see 3:9–10).

- "The wages of sin is death, but the gift of God is eternal life in Christ Jesus our Lord" (Rom. 6:23).

The Apostle was equally certain, however, that Christians can and will overcome sin and death through the ministry of the Holy Spirit in their lives. Christians have the assurance of the Spirit's power to overcome sin.

Paul once again began with "therefore" in Romans 8:12. Because believers have trusted in Jesus, they now are in right standing with God and face no judgment of wrong. They have overcome sin, not by keeping the law, which no person can do, but through the death of Jesus. Jesus' death paid the price of sin and made forgiveness a reality. Because of what Christ has done, believers are no longer committed to live according to the sinful nature. They are dead to sin because the Holy Spirit now lives within them and they have assurance of resurrection with Christ (8:1–11).

> Christians have the assurance of the Spirit's power to overcome sin.

These encouraging truths promise Christians they have no obligation to live by the fleshly nature. Believers no longer have to follow sinful desires and acts. The carnal nature cannot demand evil actions and expect compliance. Sinful tendencies, although still present, can now be overcome in the Spirit (8:12).

Anyone who lives by the demands and tendencies of the sinful nature will die (be separated from God and true life; 8:13). The believer, on the other hand, can turn away from temptations to sin by relying on the Spirit's power to help him or her "put to death the misdeeds of the body." The words "put to death" carry the meaning of *stop or cease from these actions as if they were dead.* Those who die to sinful tendencies seek to treat these actions as things no longer alive.

Killing these sinful tendencies is not in human power, though. Paul taught, "If *by the Spirit* you put to death the misdeeds of the body" (8:13, italics added for emphasis). There is the answer! Only by the empowering and enabling work of the Holy Spirit can one truly die to sin. The Holy Spirit will slay these sinful practices, but the person must give the Spirit permission. To the degree that you give the Holy Spirit permission, the Spirit will put to death the sinful actions in your life.

You can have victory over sin and the flesh through the ministry of the Holy Spirit because you are a child of God and led by the Spirit of God (8:14). You must simply submit to the Spirit's influence and control. An unwillingness to submit to the influence of the Holy Spirit is one evidence of the lack of relationship with Christ.

Victory over Fear (8:15–17)

Fear and anxiety are enemies of Christian living. As believers need victory over sin, they also need triumph over fear. Freedom from fear is available through the salvation Jesus provides. The Apostle declared that believers did not receive a spirit of fear or slavery but rather "the Spirit of sonship" (8:15).

> To the degree that you give the Holy Spirit permission, the Spirit will put to death the sinful actions in your life.

How does this "Spirit of sonship" help us overcome fear? Believers can call out to God in the intimate words of address, "*Abba,* Father" (8:15). "*Abba*" is an Aramaic word that evokes the thought of our word *Daddy,* an intimate name of endearment, a name used in a close family relationship. The privilege of having a close and intimate relationship with God, knowing that God cares for us far more deeply than even the best earthly parent, helps us face and overcome our fears. Christians belong to the family of the redeemed, of whom God is the Father and Protector. We can call God *"Abba,"* Daddy.

Facing Life's Challenges

Picture two people facing a similar challenge, in which the outcome is out of their hands. Perhaps it is a matter of health—their own or that of someone dear to them. Perhaps it is some other serious challenge. One person is fearful and distraught, filled with anxiety, worried about what might happen. The other is fully aware of the challenge but is at peace, expressing trust in a loving God.

Which of these is safe in God's care? Actually, both might well be safe in God's care. Nothing could take them from God's care and protection. But isn't it better to live life with a sense of the assurance of God's care than in a perpetual state of fear, anxiety, and worry?

We can count on God, and we have no need to be anxious or fearful in facing life's challenges. What does this passage suggest that might help someone you know—perhaps you—face life's challenges with more of a sense of assurance and hope?

Being adopted into the very family of God with this close relationship with God means, too, that believers are heirs of God and co-heirs of Christ. They will without doubt share in Christ's sufferings in this world, but they will as certainly share in Christ's glory (8:16–17).

God will care for us even more than a loving parent cares for his or her child. The Christian life means victory over fear!

Victory over Trials (8:18–39)

Along with the victories over sin and fear, the Christian life includes victory over trials. As with all people, Christians face trials and sufferings. Some of the trials come as the consequence of living in a fallen world marred by sin. Some trials arise because of the direct action of those who oppose God and God's people. Some arise because of the bad decisions of Christians themselves. (Sadly, we are not immune to making bad decisions.) Whatever the source, Christians face trials and sufferings but face them with the conscious assurance that in Jesus they can experience victory.

> *God will care for us even more than a loving parent cares for his or her child.*

Paul taught that even in hardships, Christians will receive renewal, freedom, and restoration as members of God's family. Paul declared (8:18) that he considered the present sufferings not comparable to the glory that Christians will share with Christ. Paul was not minimizing the difficulty of present-day sufferings. The Apostle had seen his share of hardships in following Christ (see, for example, Acts 14:19–29). Even so, Paul believed and taught that Christians would be victorious. The sufferings they experienced were "not worth comparing with the glory that will be revealed in us" (Rom. 8:18).

> *We can walk through great trials with full confidence that the Lord is with us and will empower us for living victoriously in spite of any circumstance.*

In the next verse, Romans 8:19, Paul painted this picture on an even larger canvas. The consequences of sin had affected not only people but also the entire creation (see Genesis 3:18–19). So, Paul said, creation itself looks forward to being "liberated from its bondage to decay and brought into the glorious freedom of the children of God" (Rom. 8:21). The creation "has been groaning" (8:22), expressing pain as a woman in childbirth. That is, creation itself was suffering pain as in the birth process, but deliverance was certain. As the mother rejoiced after the birth of the new child, then believers and creation, who together "groan" (8:23), will together rejoice at the new life.

The saved "have the firstfruits of the Spirit" (8:23). The image "firstfruits" portrays the beginnings of the harvest, with the full glorious harvest to come (8:19–23). As creation awaits and longs for liberation from decay (8:21), believers await the final adoption, the act of being brought into God's family in "hope" that the full glorious experience God has in store will come (8:24–25).

As believers patiently await the fulfillment of this hope, they do not always know how to pray. We sometimes "do not know what we ought to pray for" (8:26). The Spirit, though, "helps us in our weakness" (8:26), expressing the content of our prayers. The Spirit knows the hearts of believers and makes intercession for Christians, even when they do not know how to pray (8:27).

Believers can also have this victory over trials when they realize that a loving God will make good come from even our most distressing circumstances. Romans 8:28 is a treasure, offering comfort in the most difficult of circumstances. In that verse Paul declared that "in all things"—the good and the bad, the hard and the easy, the happy and the sad, health and sickness, prosperity and poverty, calm and storm—"God works for the good of those who love him." Recall that centuries earlier Joseph had said to his brothers that they had intended to do evil to him but God had meant and used it for good (Gen. 50:20).

> *. . . Believers have the assurance of knowing that nothing can separate them from their God.*

Once I shared with a deacon a decision I had made. This godly person taught me much when he said that the great thing about being a Christian was you could seek God's will, do it, and then look back in years to come and see that you had done the right thing. Christians can trust God in their trials and then look back to see God bringing good out of the most trying of experiences. When we trust even our most serious trials to God, God will bring good out of these situations.

Victory over trials comes, too, as we recognize and experience God's continued presence and protection of his own. In Romans 8:30, we meet the idea of predestination. In the context of this verse, predestination means that when God calls a person, God will see that person through.

God predestinates, calls, justifies, and glorifies, that is, brings to full development (8:30).

In the rich and encouraging words of Romans 8:31–39, we see that believers have the assurance of knowing that nothing can separate them from their God. Since God "did not spare his own Son, but gave him up for us all" (8:32), we can rest assured that God will freely provide everything else we need.

We can trust fully in God to provide victory over sin, assurance in times of anxiety and fear, and peace in the midst of trials and sufferings.

In verse 36, Paul quoted Psalm 44:22 to show that God's people have long suffered persecution and difficulty but they can count on the God of love to see his people through (8:31–39). God has declared believers to be in right standing with him, and nothing can separate them from God. So Romans 8:31–39 teaches us.

Summary

God's people are assured victory in the face of any trials or persecutions. The Holy Spirit indwells believers and guides them to victory over sin, fear, and trials. We can walk through great trials with full confidence that the Lord is with us and will empower us for living victoriously in spite of any circumstance.

Applying These Truths

1. What is true victory in life? Is victory outscoring someone? Is it making the greatest profit? Is it gaining the highest reputation? Or is it serving God and others? We should rethink our concept of victory. We should consider victory to be living in God's care and by God's plan and serving God by reaching out to others.
2. We can trust fully in God to provide victory over sin, assurance in times of anxiety and fear, and peace in the midst of trials and sufferings.

QUESTIONS

1. What temptations are most serious in your life? How can you allow the Holy Spirit to guide you through these temptations?

2. Have you attempted to change some habit or way of acting and failed? Could the problem be that you are acting out of human strength rather than allowing the Spirit to put to death the deeds of the human nature?

3. How do you handle fear and anxiety? Are you often anxious over health, money, the welfare of your family, or other matters? What does the privilege of calling God *"Abba*, Father" suggest about dealing with our fears?

4. What difficulties are you facing? What implications for living does this passage of Scripture have for you as you face them?

NOTES

1. ABC Television's *Wide World of Sports*.

Continuing to Care for the Jewish People

Unit three, "Continuing to Care for the Jewish People," is a one-lesson study of Romans 9—11. This unit continues the theme of Romans, "What God Is Up To." These chapters begin with Paul's anguish that his own people had rejected the Messiah and the Christian way. As Romans 9—11 concludes, Paul communicated his assured belief that God would fulfill his covenants and continue to love and offer salvation to the Jewish people.

Romans 9—11 do not promise salvation to each and every Israelite. Neither do they relate directly to the present national state of Israel. Rather the Apostle presented the fact that Israel, the religious people, is different from the political nation-state. The chapters express the conviction that God in his faithfulness continues to offer salvation to all people, including Jews who will turn to him through Christ.[1]

UNIT THREE. CONTINUING TO CARE FOR THE JEWISH PEOPLE

Lesson 10	What About the Jewish People?	Romans 9:1–7; 10:1–13; 11:1–2a, 25–32

NOTES

1. Unless otherwise indicated, all Scripture quotations in unit three, lesson ten, are from the New International Version.

Focal Text

Romans 9:1–7; 10:1–13;
11:1–2a, 25–32

Background

Romans 9—11

Main Idea

God continues to offer
salvation to all people,
Jews as well as Gentiles.

Question to Explore

What is God's approach
to the Jewish people now?

Study Aim

To trace Paul's discussion of God's dealings
with the Jewish people and to summarize what
it teaches about relating to Jewish people today

Study and Action Emphases

- Affirm the Bible as our authoritative guide for
  life and ministry
- Share the gospel with all people
- Develop a growing, vibrant faith
- Value all people as created in the image of
  God

LESSON TEN

What About the Jewish People?

Quick Read

Those who as the Jewish people of Paul's day
seek to earn salvation through keeping the law
will fail. The only way to right standing with
God is through faith in Jesus Christ. God keeps
his promises to save all who believe.

Within minutes of being seated beside a young man on an airplane flight, I learned he lived in a town near Nazareth in Israel, was in the United States to buy computers, and was a devoted follower of Judaism. He was not offended as I shared my faith.

The young man explained his reasons for not considering Christianity. High among these was his belief that when Messiah came, everyone would recognize him, believe him, acknowledge him, and follow him. No one would doubt Messiah when he came. He explained, "Since I doubt Jesus was Messiah, Jesus could not be Messiah, for all will accept him when he comes."

Nothing changed his conviction. We parted—I in disappointment and my young acquaintance still trapped in the darkness of his doubt that Jesus is the Messiah.

My last question and his answer remains with me. I asked, "Do you still look for Messiah?"

With tears on his cheeks, he responded, "Every day I look for Messiah. Every day I pray for Messiah."

What is God's will for Jewish people today? How does God deal with Jewish people today? The Apostle answered in his Letter to the Romans, chapters 9—11. He emphasized:

- God continues to offer salvation to all, Jews and Gentiles alike
- God keeps his covenants and promises
- God longs for the salvation of all people, including Jewish people

Romans 9:1–7

[1]I speak the truth in Christ—I am not lying, my conscience confirms it in the Holy Spirit—[2]I have great sorrow and unceasing anguish in my heart. [3]For I could wish that I myself were cursed and cut off from Christ for the sake of my brothers, those of my own race, [4]the people of Israel. Theirs is the adoption as sons; theirs the divine glory, the covenants, the receiving of the law, the temple worship and the promises. [5]Theirs are the patriarchs, and from them is traced the human ancestry of Christ, who is God over all, forever praised! Amen.

[6]It is not as though God's word had failed. For not all who are descended from Israel are Israel. [7]Nor because they are his descendants are they all Abraham's children. On the contrary, "It is through Isaac that your offspring will be reckoned."

Romans 10:1–13

¹Brothers, my heart's desire and prayer to God for the Israelites is that they may be saved. **²**For I can testify about them that they are zealous for God, but their zeal is not based on knowledge. **³**Since they did not know the righteousness that comes from God and sought to establish their own, they did not submit to God's righteousness. **⁴**Christ is the end of the law so that there may be righteousness for everyone who believes.

⁵Moses describes in this way the righteousness that is by the law: "The man who does these things will live by them." **⁶**But the righteousness that is by faith says: "Do not say in your heart, 'Who will ascend into heaven?'" (that is, to bring Christ down) **⁷**"or 'Who will descend into the deep?'" (that is, to bring Christ up from the dead). **⁸**But what does it say? "The word is near you; it is in your mouth and in your heart," that is, the word of faith we are proclaiming: **⁹**That if you confess with your mouth, "Jesus is Lord," and believe in your heart that God raised him from the dead, you will be saved. **¹⁰**For it is with your heart that you believe and are justified, and it is with your mouth that you confess and are saved. **¹¹**As the Scripture says, "Anyone who trusts in him will never be put to shame." **¹²**For there is no difference between Jew and Gentile—the same Lord is Lord of all and richly blesses all who call on him, **¹³**for, "Everyone who calls on the name of the Lord will be saved."

Romans 11:1–2a, 25–32

¹I ask then: Did God reject his people? By no means! I am an Israelite myself, a descendant of Abraham, from the tribe of Benjamin. **²**God did not reject his people, whom he foreknew.

. . . .

²⁵I do not want you to be ignorant of this mystery, brothers, so that you may not be conceited: Israel has experienced a hardening in part until the full number of the Gentiles has come in. **²⁶**And so all Israel will be saved, as it is written:
"The deliverer will come from Zion;
   he will turn godlessness away from Jacob.
²⁷ And this is my covenant with them
   when I take away their sins."
²⁸As far as the gospel is concerned, they are enemies on your account; but as far as election is concerned, they are loved on account of the

patriarchs, **29**for God's gifts and his call are irrevocable. **30**Just as you who were at one time disobedient to God have now received mercy as a result of their disobedience, **31**so they too have now become disobedient in order that they too may now receive mercy as a result of God's mercy to you. **32**For God has bound all men over to disobedience so that he may have mercy on them all.

God's Desire for All People (9:1–7)

Chapters 9—11 are vital and integral parts of Romans. They form the perfect bridge from the accounts of God's provision of salvation (Romans 1—8) and the teachings about salvation's outworking in believers (Rom. 12—16).

In Romans 9—11, Paul addressed two central questions—(1) the rejection of God's Messiah by many Jews and (2) doubts of some concerning the faithfulness of God to his promises. The

God keeps his covenants.

Apostle called on Gentile Christians not to consider the Israelites beyond God's care or reach. Romans 1—8 established that God's promises are available to all people, Jew and non-Jew alike. Romans 9—11 will establish that God's faithfulness still reaches to the people of Israel. God is not unfaithful. God keeps his covenants.

In Romans 9:1, Paul revealed his heart, stating that his "conscience" was clear about his anguish for his people, the Jews. Perhaps part of the background for this statement was Paul's insistence that he was not preaching to Gentiles because of indifference or hostility toward the Jews. Rather, Paul expressed his great emotional distress over the rejection of God's way by many Jews. Such a feeling was often expressed in the Old Testament (see Jeremiah 4:19–22).

The Apostle expressed the depth of his feeling by stating that he could even wish he could be separated from Christ for the sake of his people, the Jews. Paul knew that such a sacrifice could not bring any to salvation, though. Like Moses (Exodus 32:32), Paul longed to stand between and serve as the bridge between God and his people.

When Paul spoke of his people, he called them "the people of Israel," the NIV translation of the Greek word *Israelites* (Rom. 9:4). The word *Israelites* was a more religious term than the term *Jews* used earlier in

Romans. By using *Israelites*, Paul may have been signaling his intention to consider more directly the religious position of the people and their position before God. *Israelites* came from the name God bestowed on Jacob (Genesis 32:28; 35:10) and passed on to Jacob's offspring (Gen. 32:32; 46:8). Thus the term *Israelite* hints at the favored status of this people.

Paul pointed to the advantages that God had given the Israelites (Rom. 9:4–5). They had received the "adoption," that is, God's selection to receive his covenant and act as the conduit of his blessings. Too, the Israelites had experienced the "glory" of God, that is, God's presence, especially in the temple. Also, they had received the "covenants," probably the promises to Abraham (Gen. 12) and to David (2 Samuel 7). Too,

> *Paul taught that what counts is grace and not race.*

they had received "the law" and the blessings of "temple worship and the promises." Further, they had followed the "patriarchs." As the greatest of blessings, God had delivered his promise of Messiah, Jesus Christ, through the lineage of the Israelites.

In Romans 9:6, Paul defended God's faithfulness to his promises to Israel. The Apostle taught in that verse that God never promised salvation to every individual Jew. By saying, "For not all who are descended from Israel are Israel" (9:6), Paul attested that salvation comes through faith in Christ, not through physical birth.

The Apostle differed from Jewish ideas that God's covenant with Abraham guaranteed salvation to every Jew who had not renounced the law. Paul taught that what counts is grace and not race. These verses declare that God still desires and is able to save all who believe, including those from the Jewish people who repent.

The Reason for Lostness and the Path to Salvation (10:1–13)

Paul introduced the teachings of chapter 10 in Romans 9:30–33. He dealt with the facts that many Jews were rejecting Jesus as Messiah and Gentiles were turning to Christ. Many Israelites were trying to earn right standing with God rather than accepting God's offer of righteousness. They had "pursued" right standing with God by means of keeping the law but had not achieved this status in that manner (9:31).

The Testimony to Christ's Divinity in Romans 9:5

The New International Version translates Romans 9:5 in this manner: "Theirs are the patriarchs, and from them is traced the human ancestry of *Christ, who is God over all, forever praised! Amen*" (italics added for emphasis). Note that this verse attributes the title "God" to Jesus and thus explicitly confirms Jesus' deity.

Paul pointed to two Old Testament references to stones of stumbling (Isaiah 8:14; 28:16). Jesus used the image of the stone also (Matthew 21:42). The idea is that the Jews stumbled over Christ, the real way to right standing with God, and sought righteousness by law-keeping. Faith in Jesus thus became a stumbling block for them.

Paul commended the Israelites' "zeal" to keep the law (Rom. 10:1–2). "Zeal" was a prized virtue among the Jews during the period between the testaments because it involved protecting Israel from corruption. The Jews' zeal was, however, misdirected. They were striving to earn their righteousness rather than subjecting themselves to God's promise of right-standing in Christ (10:3). In Philippians 3:6–9, Paul traced his own experience of striving by works to earn righteousness and then turning to receive God's gift by faith.

> *So the genuine way to right standing with God is through repentance, confession, and faith (Rom. 10:9–10).*

In Romans 10:4, Paul wrote, "Christ is the end of the law." Picture a race in which the runner reaches the finish line, the goal. The runner crossing the finish line marks the end of the race but also the purpose of running. God intended all along to complete the law in Christ. Jesus is the end of the law's rule even as he begins the time of fulfillment to which the law pointed.

In Romans 10:5, Paul quoted Leviticus 18:5, "The man who does these things will live by them." This verse was not saying that through obedience to the law the Jews would attain salvation but that by keeping the law they would enjoy the benefits of the Promised Land. Paul then contrasted the righteousness by faith with this earned righteousness (10:6–8). Using phrases from Deuteronomy 30:11–14, Paul declared that the righteousness based on faith is the "word" that is present and accessible. No one had to go into heaven or travel to the depths to secure it. Christ already had brought this salvation and made it available.

So the genuine way to right standing with God is through repentance, confession, and faith (Rom. 10:9–10). No one who came to God in faith would ever be "put to shame," that is, never be subject to a negative verdict (10:11; see Isa. 28:16). In Romans 10:13, the idea of "calls on the name of" was a usual way of speaking of asking assistance, usually from a god. The use of the term "Lord" in reference to Jesus stresses Jesus' deity.

In these verses Paul proclaimed the essence of the gospel. The Apostle clarified the basics of Christianity, which involves salvation by faith in the life, death, and resurrection of Jesus. The gospel proclaims that no difference exists between people. All, Jew and Gentile, remain under the power of sin until released from this bondage by salvation. The one God blesses all who call on him; everyone who calls on him will be saved.

The Assurance of God's Promises (11:1–2, 25–32)

In chapter 11, Paul returned to his theme of 9:6–29. He had spoken about why many Jews rejected the Messiah and many Gentiles accepted him. He declared that in spite of Israel's disobedience (10:21), God had not rejected the people of Israel (11:2). Many through rejecting Messiah had been hardened, that is, they had been turned away from the Lord by their stubborn rejection of his grace (11:7). Still, a "remnant" (11:5), the "elect" (11:7), had trusted Christ and received God's promise.

Paul repeated the point of Romans 10:19–20, that repentance and faith had come to the Gentiles to make Israel "envious" (10:19; see Deut. 32:21). The word "envious" does not suggest that God had sinful attitudes or actions. Rather, Paul was teaching that the Gentiles coming to faith would stimulate the Jews to return to their God and his salvation (Rom. 11:11–15).

The Apostle clarified the basics of Christianity, which involves salvation by faith in the life, death, and resurrection of Jesus.

In 11:16–17, the Apostle used two illustrations of how Jews and Gentiles were related to God's overall purpose for humankind. First, Paul referred to the portion of the dough that is offered as firstfruits. It makes the entire batch "holy," or set apart to God (11:16). The "firstfruits" refers to the Jews. Second, Paul referred to the wild branches grafted onto the olive tree. The Gentile believers were the wild branches that had been grafted into the Jewish olive tree.

When a branch was grafted onto a tree, the branch received nourishment and strength from the tree to which it was joined. In his illustration, Paul reversed the usual method of grafting good branches onto a tree. So Paul's illustration affirmed the place of the Jews. The Apostle's point was that the message came first to the Jews but upon their rejection moved to the Gentiles. It would someday return to Israel (11:22–24).

God desires the salvation of both Jews and Gentiles.

In verse 25 Paul explained salvation history by calling it a "mystery" (a matter not previously understood but now by revelation made clear). He said that the hardening of Israel would continue until the full number of Gentles came into God's kingdom.

In verse 26, Paul stated directly, "so all Israel will be saved." What does this statement mean? My interpretation is that the Apostle was speaking of Israel in a collective sense rather than saying that every individual Jew would be saved. Such use of "all Israel" can be seen in Joshua 7:25 and 2 Samuel 16:22 where "all Israel" means the people in general rather than each and every Israelite. Romans 11:26 thus promises that a representative number of the Jews will find Jesus as Messiah.

The only way to gain peace with God and right standing with him is by faith.

Paul was convinced that God would honor his promises based on his covenants. God's promises are unchangeable. In previous times, both Gentiles and Jews were disobedient. God, though, worked to show mercy to both groups (11:28–30). God "has bound all men over to disobedience" (11:32; that is, *locked all in the prison of disobedience*) that he might show mercy to all.

Paul concluded this section with a great doxology of praise to God (11:33–36). He expressed praise for the God who offers salvation to all, Jews and Gentiles.

Summary

God desires the salvation of both Jews and Gentiles. In spite of God's desire for all to be saved, though, many reject the Messiah and thus are lost. The Jews tried to earn right standing with God by keeping the law, but gaining right standing with God in this way is impossible. The only way to gain peace with God and right standing with him is by faith. Although many Jews for whom the Apostle longed were lost, God would continue to offer salvation to all who would come to faith in Christ.

Applying These Truths

Christians should apply these truths by

- Trusting in God's faithfulness to keep his covenants and promises
- Continuing to pray for Jewish people and engage in efforts to lead them to salvation in Christ
- Resisting any prejudices against Jewish people
- Refusing to make these verses political statements in present-day conflicts

QUESTIONS

1. What do you think Paul meant when he said, "all Israel will be saved" (Rom. 11:26)?

2. Why had so many of the Jewish people of Paul's day refused to accept Christ?

3. What incentives to witness to all people do you see in these verses?

4. What are some teachings in this passage that will be helpful to you in relating to Jewish people?

Calling for Faithful Living

"Dear Abby," the popular newspaper feature, provides advice on many subjects. As the "Dear Abby" website notes, Abby usually succeeds in answering calls for help with "uncommon common sense."

The Apostle Paul also approached problems and issues with "uncommon common sense." As far as we know, the Christians in Rome never wrote a "Dear Paul" letter requesting advice. If they had, though, the note might have read something like this:

Dear Paul,

We only recently returned to Rome after being expelled by the Emperor Claudius. Our church has many new converts, both Jewish and Gentile. We have varied backgrounds, traditions, and points of view. Many of us have strong opinions that clash. A few don't even want to pay taxes. How do we get along with one another and with the government, especially since we desire to draw others to Christ and don't want to be expelled again?

In Christus,
Lucius Aurelius

In Romans 12—15, the passages studied in unit four, we find Paul's response as he offers guidance on living as followers of Christ in the church and in the world. In lesson eleven, the Apostle called Christians to "Live in Response to God's Mercy," using their gifts effectively in Christ's service. In lesson twelve, Paul described how to "Live Like This" in relationships with other believers, governmental authorities, and the greater community. Finally, in lesson thirteen,

Paul told the Roman Christians to "Welcome Christians with Whom You Disagree" and learn to live in unity. These lessons deal with Paul's instructions on how to live in light of the great theological truths of the preceding chapters.

As I read and reread these passages and studied various commentaries on them, I squirmed. God used the Letter to the Romans to insist I re-examine how I live as a Christian in my church and in my world. As you study these lessons, carefully consider how Paul's practical, pertinent advice and admonitions to the Christians of his day pertain to you and your church today.[1]

UNIT FOUR. CALLING FOR FAITHFUL LIVING

NOTES

1. Unless otherwise indicated, all Scripture quotations in unit four, lessons eleven through thirteen, are from the New International Version.

Focal Text

Romans 12:1–8

Background

Romans 12:1–8

Main Idea

God's great mercy in our lives calls us to give ourselves wholly to God, using our gifts in serving God and one another.

Question to Explore

To what extent have you given yourself to God, using your gifts in humbly serving God and other people?

Study Aim

To decide on ways I will give myself to God in response to God's great mercy to me

Study and Action Emphases

- Affirm the Bible as our authoritative guide for life and ministry
- Share the gospel with all people
- Develop a growing, vibrant faith
- Include all God's family in decision-making and service
- Value all people as created in the image of God
- Obey and serve Jesus by meeting physical, spiritual, and emotional needs
- Equip people for servant leadership

LESSON ELEVEN

Live in Response to God's Mercy

Quick Read

Paul calls Christians individually to live sacrificially according to God's transforming grace and collectively to live in harmony within the church, realistically and effectively using their gifts in God's service.

Shortly after earning my degree, I found myself standing on the chalkboard side of the teacher's desk. Anyone wandering the halls heard groans when I announced, "Today we're going to diagram sentences." I didn't understand the reason for the groans. My elegant sixth-grade teacher had introduced me to the exercise, and I enjoyed examining each word in each sentence. I quickly learned one of Mrs. Bowen's crucial lessons, "Seemingly insignificant words can be significant." The meanings of entire sentences or whole stories often hinge on one tiny word such as *if* or *after*.

Paul used a hinge word as he changed focus in Romans. He chose the word "therefore" to shift from the theological insights in Romans 1—11 to the practical instruction in Romans 12—16 (Romans 12:1). Paul could have used *consequently*, *for these reasons*, or *thus*. But he made the transition with a word that carries a double meaning—as a consequence and as introducing a logical conclusion. As Christians we strive to live in a Christlike manner as both consequence of and logical conclusion to our acceptance of God's mercies—God's forgiveness, grace, and salvation through the death of Jesus Christ.

Simply put, in these verses, Paul emphasized that our beliefs must affect our behavior. Our lives must prove our faith. Paul explained how.

Romans 12:1–8

1Therefore, I urge you, brothers, in view of God's mercy, to offer your bodies as living sacrifices, holy and pleasing to God—this is your spiritual act of worship. **2**Do not conform any longer to the pattern of this world, but be transformed by the renewing of your mind. Then you will be able to test and approve what God's will is—his good, pleasing and perfect will.

3For by the grace given me I say to every one of you: Do not think of yourself more highly than you ought, but rather think of yourself with sober judgment, in accordance with the measure of faith God has given you. **4**Just as each of us has one body with many members, and these members do not all have the same function, **5**so in Christ we who are many form one body, and each member belongs to all the others. **6**We have different gifts, according to the grace given us. If a man's gift is prophesying, let him use it in proportion to his faith. **7**If it is serving, let him serve; if it is teaching, let him teach; **8**if it is encouraging, let him encourage; if it is contributing to the needs of others, let him give generously; if it is leadership, let him govern diligently; if it is showing mercy, let him do it cheerfully.

Every Moment, Every Day, Live Sacrificially (12:1–2)

Recently we attended the wedding of a Naval Academy graduate preparing to become a SEAL. He was in superb physical condition. We wondered why everyone offered him ice cream, cookies, and chips. Then we learned that he faced intensive training—training that would simulate survival situations from being captured by an enemy to crashing in remote locations, training that would result in significant weight loss. I rejoiced that Brandon would willingly offer himself as a living sacrifice for his country. Such sacrifice could only be born of deep love and devotion.

Paul understood that kind of deep love and devotion. He considered himself "poured out like a drink offering" (2 Timothy 4:6). In Romans 1—11, the Apostle explained God's mercy as the reason for his feelings. Then, in Romans 12:1–8, he urged others who experienced the grace of salvation to offer themselves willingly to God. Paul's urging doesn't imply begging or options or asking with a "pretty please with cream and sugar on top." Instead, he implored in a way similar to the parent who commands, *Buckle your seatbelt.* As Christians, we don't have a choice. Because of Christ's death, we must offer our "bodies as living sacrifices, holy and pleasing to God" (Rom. 12:1).

Personal sacrifice doesn't appeal to most Americans, and we possess little experience with religious sacrifice. I've never seen an animal sacrifice except on slides by friends who serve among Hindus. But the early Christians understood sacrifice as part of worship. In the Old Testament, God told Abraham to sacrifice his son Isaac (Genesis 22:2). In Exodus, God commanded the Israelites to sacrifice perfect year-old male sheep or goats. The Israelites then were to paint their doorframes with the blood to save their firstborn (Exodus 12:1–30). In Leviticus, God provided laws governing sacrifices. But God also told the prophet Hosea to warn the people that God desired actions more than sacrifices (Hosea 6:6).

Paul's audience knew that sacrifices had to be perfect, holy, and offered with the right attitude. Therefore, in light of Christ's death on the cross that eliminated the need for animal sacrifices, our only response can be offering ourselves intelligently, willingly, and with dedication to God's service every moment. Or as Jesus urged, we must love the Lord with all our hearts, souls, and minds (Matthew 22:37). That is our spiritual worship, worship that involves not just a few hours each week but the totality of who we are and how we act all the time. Christianity shouldn't be just our religion. Christianity must be our life. But how?

Our daughter Holly teaches first grade, including a boy-popular unit, "Bugs, Butterflies, and Other Creepy-Crawlies." In one lesson, the children paste rice and different pastas on paper to show the sequence of metamorphosis: egg, caterpillar, cocoon, and butterfly. Ideally, the children also watch a butterfly emerge from its cocoon and fly into the sky. But metamorphosis doesn't just happen with butterflies.

Paul's audience knew that sacrifices had to be perfect, holy, and offered with the right attitude.

God's mercies lead to transformation in lives. The verb "transformed" carries the idea of change. Gospel writers used the same verb in describing the transfiguration of Jesus (Matt. 17:2; Mark 9:2).

But this transformation isn't once and for all. It isn't magical. It's hard work. Like the butterfly that struggles to free itself from the cocoon, we struggle to free ourselves from the effects of the world. Paul warned that we should not "conform . . . to the pattern of this world" (Rom. 12:2). The verb translated "conform" indicates being shaped or molded. Peter used the same word in 1 Peter 1:14, " . . . do not conform to the evil desires. . . ." We shouldn't be Jell-O® molded by the world.

The move from conforming to being transformed occurs through the "renewing of your mind" (Rom. 12:2). How do we renew our minds? Through an ongoing, internal process that changes how we think. A world filled with words and images opposed to Christ's words and images makes life difficult. But when we accept Christ, the Holy Spirit resides within

Our lives must prove our faith.

us. The Holy Spirit, along with the Bible and gifted teachers, puts God's ideas and thoughts into our minds. Christ's church also offers help and encouragement.

Only when we willingly sacrifice ourselves and are transformed through a renewed mind can we "test and approve what God's will is—his good, pleasing and perfect will" (12:2). The idea is to prove through testing.

Serving as a Baylor University librarian puts me in contact with college students seeking God's will. Sometimes I'm amazed. One told me that since she made a *B* in pre-med biology, becoming a doctor wasn't "God's will." Maybe, but maybe she needs to study harder. Discovering God's will may require trying and testing. The world's will is not God's will. A preacher friend says that if it isn't in the character of Christ, it isn't in the heart of God. If it isn't in the heart of God, it isn't in his will. And if it is God's perfect will, we will desire that will.

Every Moment, Every Day, Live Realistically (12:3)

I couldn't wait to go off to college. I loved my professors. I even loved cafeteria food. I especially loved my new Sunday dress. That first Lord's day, I bounded out of bed, curled my hair, applied make-up, and donned the dress. On my way to church, I admired myself in the glass door as I exited the dormitory. I promptly crashed knees first down the steps, scraping my shins and bleeding on my new dress. Reality crashed in, too, as I headed upstairs for a change after my pride fell along with my fall.

> *Because of Christ's death, we must offer our "bodies as living sacrifices, holy and pleasing to God" (Rom. 12:1).*

Paul says we need that change, too, from pride to "sober judgment" (12:3). In verse 3, the Apostle moved from concern for the individual as an individual to concern for the individual within the Christian community. After reminding the Romans of his authority, the

Spiritual Gifts in the Bible

Although we think of *prophecy* as foretelling, Old Testament prophets from Miriam (Exodus 15:20) to Malachi clearly spoke revelations from God related to everyday life, preaching with power and passion.

The one whom God graces with *service* often does so behind the scenes with caring, consistency, and calmness like Dorcas (Acts 9:36–41) and Stephen (Acts 6:1–6).

Gifted *teachers* study and communicate God's truths in words that touch hearts and change lives. Apollos met master teachers in Ephesus—Priscilla and Aquila (Acts 18:24–26).

Encouragers, like Barnabas who counseled John Mark (Acts 15:36–40) and like Mary who anointed Jesus (John 12:1–3), support others in their times of difficulty, weakness, or vulnerability.

Some Christians, like the widow with her mite (Luke 21:1–4) and like Nicodemus (John 19:38–42), *give* generously and joyfully beyond God's requirements.

Leaders organize and direct God's work efficiently and effectively. Deborah led diligently (Judges 4). So did Joshua (Joshua 1:1–15).

A Christian with *mercy* lives with compellingly positive compassion, especially for the unloved. The servant girl of Naaman's wife helped a leper (2 Kings 5:1–14). Elijah acted mercifully toward the widow at Zarephath (1 Kings 17:7–24).

Apostle offered sound advice. We should have neither too high nor too low an opinion of ourselves. Instead, we must judge ourselves realistically in proportion to the faith provided us to perform our God-given responsibilities—not an easy task. The Christian community doesn't have room for egos. Neither does it have space for those who cower in the corner. Healthy pride serves God. False pride serves the world.

Every Moment, Every Day, Live Loyally (12:4–5)

I grew up in the country, a quarter-mile from our nearest neighbors. I loved spending time in the Blaylock's home. Mabel's kitchen always smelled of fresh-baked goodies, and Billy Frank made everything fun. Billy Frank had fought in World War II, losing his leg when wounded a few feet from and just moments before the photographer shot the famous photo of "Raising Flag on Mount Suribachi" on February 23,

God's mercies lead to transformation in lives.

1945. Billy Frank managed to save one leg by applying a tourniquet but couldn't save the other. I think of him and his missing leg whenever I read Paul's comparison of the parts of the human body to the members of Christ's church (12:4–5). Billy Frank functioned without his leg but not as he had functioned with it. Paul knew that with the absence, idleness, or indifference of one of its members, the church would function, but not as well.

In the human body, the heart can't substitute for a lung or the liver for a kidney. Children learn that eyes and ears control two of the five senses, but neither tastes, smells, nor feels. Yet, they all work together to form one body. To borrow the motto by Alexandre Dumas in *The Three Musketeers,* they're "one for all, and all for one." They give their all and stay loyal to each other "through thick and thin."

We should have neither too high nor too low an opinion of ourselves.

That's how Paul described the church, not only in his Letter to the Romans, but also to the Colossians (Col. 1:18), to the Corinthians (1 Corinthians 12:12–27), and to the Ephesians (Ephesians 4:16). Christ heads the church. Then together individual Christians unite to accomplish God's work on earth. God's call to service is both-and, individual and shared.

The Church: Many Members, One Body

First Church, Anytown, recently realized that less than one-fourth of its active members participate beyond attending worship services and sitting in Sunday School classes.

Consider some of the reasons. What advice would you offer? What strategies would you recommend to help all members identify and use their spiritual gifts to build up the church?

My husband likes to use the sports team analogy for the body of Christ where every player from quarterback to kicker in football, from catcher to designated hitter in baseball, and from point to post in basketball has a unique but important role to play. Those players aren't uniform, except in their clothing. They're unified.

Every Moment, Every Day, Live Effectively (12:7–8)

Consider the care with which you choose a gift for someone who is special to you and to whom you want to show your love. When we become part of God's family, God carefully selects the perfect spiritual gift(s) for us. We receive "different gifts, according to the grace given us" (Rom. 12:6). In Romans, Paul chose a sampling strongly related to church life and addressed the use of each separately: prophe-

Christianity shouldn't be just our religion. Christianity must be our life.

sying, serving, teaching, encouraging, contributing, leading, and showing mercy (12:7–8). In 1 Corinthians, Paul offered another list (1 Cor. 12). In Ephesians, he told how Christ "gave some to be apostles, some to be prophets, some to be evangelists, and some to be pastors and teachers" (Eph. 4:11). Peter mentioned speaking and serving (1 Pet. 4:10–11).

God evidently didn't intend for any of the scriptural lists to be exhaustive. Yet all have commonalities. They all state the source of gifts as God. They all note the importance of these gifts in building up the church. They all demonstrate variety. They all indicate that Christians possess at least one gift. They all offer the expectation that each Christian utilize his or her gift(s). The church isn't dependent on one or a few special people. No gift is *the* gift. They're presents from God. Just as we would never pass a birthday without opening and enjoying a beautifully wrapped gift, so we should open, enjoy, and share our spiritual gifts. We abuse them through disuse.

But how do I know my gift(s)? In *Yours for the Giving*, Barbara Joiner offered an inventory.[1] After attending her conference, I realized that others saw my gifts more clearly than I and that my gifts encompassed my passions and abilities. God gives us the deep desire and unyielding yearning to express ourselves through our gifts.

Every Moment, Every Day, Live Responsively

For years I exercised my gifts leading Girls in Action. Every December, we invited the boys to join our mission study. One year missionaries to Africa offered a lesson about poverty. The couple equated world hunger to M&Ms®, placing candies in envelopes according to the percentage of people in a region or country who were starving, facing daily hunger, having sufficient food, or enjoying abundance. Many envelopes held just one M&M, some three, others ten, and a few barely closed. We distributed the envelopes randomly and explained about hunger. Finally, we gave permission to eat. Only one, the tiniest boy, opened his bulging envelope and shared. When he finished, we realized he hadn't eaten a single M&M. When asked why, the lad answered, "That's what it means to be a Christian."

> *God gives us the deep desire and unyielding yearning to express ourselves through our gifts.*

Do we know what it means to be a Christian, daily offering ourselves as holy, living sacrifices? Do we do what culture dictates? Or do we live transformed by God's mercy? Do we act according to God's perfect will, without false pride? Do we use our spiritual gifts to unify and build the church?

A pastor friend compares the Christian life to music. As much as we enjoy listening to a solo, the melody lacks rich harmony. As individuals in the church, we must sing together, sacrificing solos to add the richness of many voices performing God's glorious composition.

QUESTIONS

1. What are some ways we can offer ourselves daily as holy, pleasing sacrifices to God?

2. How can we avoid being conformed to our culture?

3. Can you recall a time you absolutely knew God's perfect will? How were you sure?

4. How can the church help us live sacrificially and realistically according to God's perfect will?

5. Prayerfully identify your spiritual gift(s). Ask a trusted Christian friend to help, if necessary. What are some ways you can exercise your gift(s) to build up the church? What are some ways you can encourage others to use their spiritual gifts?

NOTES

1. Barbara Joiner. *Yours for the Giving: Spiritual Gifts*. Birmingham, AL: New Hope, 1999.

Focal Text
Romans 12:9–18; 13:1–14

Background
Romans 12:9—13:14

Main Idea
Christians are to practice their faith in every area of their lives, both in and beyond the Christian community.

Question to Explore
What influences you more in how you live—your culture's practices or Christian teachings?

Study Aim
To decide on at least one imperative from these instructions for Christian living that I will put into practice

Study and Action Emphases
- Affirm the Bible as our authoritative guide for life and ministry
- Share the gospel with all people
- Develop a growing, vibrant faith
- Value all people as created in the image of God
- Obey and serve Jesus by meeting physical, spiritual, and emotional needs
- Equip people for servant leadership

LESSON TWELVE

Live Like This

Quick Read
Paul offers practical guidance for Christian relationships with other believers, governmental authorities, and neighbors.

127

As a child I loved summer camp. A myriad of activities filled the days, but mail brought a touch of home every rest hour. When I became a parent and Marshall, Michael, and Holly successively left for their camp experiences, I found myself on the other side of mail call. My husband John and I wrote every day. We filled our letters with comic strips, sports page cut-outs, and an update on Waco's searing heat. I often closed with a thought for the day, offering practical advice in phrases I hoped our offspring would remember and take to heart.

Paul wrote the same way to his children in faith, offering practical advice and guidance in living the Christian life in words he hoped they would remember and take to heart. We need to take them to heart, too.

Romans 12:9–18

[9]Love must be sincere. Hate what is evil; cling to what is good. [10]Be devoted to one another in brotherly love. Honor one another above yourselves. [11]Never be lacking in zeal, but keep your spiritual fervor, serving the Lord. [12]Be joyful in hope, patient in affliction, faithful in prayer. [13]Share with God's people who are in need. Practice hospitality.

[14]Bless those who persecute you; bless and do not curse. [15]Rejoice with those who rejoice; mourn with those who mourn. [16]Live in harmony with one another. Do not be proud, but be willing to associate with people of low position. Do not be conceited.

[17]Do not repay anyone evil for evil. Be careful to do what is right in the eyes of everybody. [18]If it is possible, as far as it depends on you, live at peace with everyone.

Romans 13:1–14

[1]Everyone must submit himself to the governing authorities, for there is no authority except that which God has established. The authorities that exist have been established by God. [2]Consequently, he who rebels against the authority is rebelling against what God has instituted, and those who do so will bring judgment on themselves. [3]For rulers hold no terror for those who do right, but for those who do wrong. Do you want to be free from fear of the one in authority? Then do what is right and he will commend you. [4]For he is God's servant to do you good. But if you do wrong, be afraid, for he does not bear the sword for nothing. He is God's servant, an agent of wrath to bring punishment on the wrongdoer.

⁵Therefore, it is necessary to submit to the authorities, not only because of possible punishment but also because of conscience.

⁶This is also why you pay taxes, for the authorities are God's servants, who give their full time to governing. ⁷Give everyone what you owe him: If you owe taxes, pay taxes; if revenue, then revenue; if respect, then respect; if honor, then honor.

⁸Let no debt remain outstanding, except the continuing debt to love one another, for he who loves his fellowman has fulfilled the law. ⁹The commandments, "Do not commit adultery," "Do not murder," "Do not steal," "Do not covet," and whatever other commandment there may be, are summed up in this one rule: "Love your neighbor as yourself." ¹⁰Love does no harm to its neighbor. Therefore love is the fulfillment of the law.

¹¹And do this, understanding the present time. The hour has come for you to wake up from your slumber, because our salvation is nearer now than when we first believed. ¹²The night is nearly over; the day is almost here. So let us put aside the deeds of darkness and put on the armor of light. ¹³Let us behave decently, as in the daytime, not in orgies and drunkenness, not in sexual immorality and debauchery, not in dissension and jealousy. ¹⁴Rather, clothe yourselves with the Lord Jesus Christ, and do not think about how to gratify the desires of the sinful nature.

Every Day, Everywhere, Live in Sincerity (12:9–21)

Paul moved from giving guidance on spiritual gifts (Romans 12:6–8) to offering advice on relationships both inside and outside the church (Rom. 12:9—13:14). In marked contrast to the first eight verses in Romans 12, the Apostle delivered ideas in quick, loosely connected sentences, each worthy of a sermon. Initially, he targeted relationships within the Christian community (12:9–13).

Paul began with a statement that brings an agreeing nod. He connected love and sincerity. Of course, we, too, say, "Love must be sincere," genuine, not fake, or it isn't love at all (12:9). Loving without hypocrisy and selfishness manifests itself in action. In the next verses, Paul described how sincere love looks.

Godly love hates evil and clings to good (12:9). The two walk hand in hand. A friend tells the story of her just-graduated-from-high-school son who responded to a call from a football teammate desperately needing a ride home from a party involving alcohol and drugs. Before her son and his best friend could extract the teammate, the police appeared and assumed the worst. Fortunately, blood tests and eyewitnesses exonerated the two young men, but the course of their lives could have been drastically altered. The mom often told her sons to run away from evil and run to good. Her son learned the lesson the hard way and realized he should have sent a cab or called his parents.

Paul urged the Roman Christians to "be devoted to one another" and "honor one another above yourselves" (12:10). "Brotherly love" encompasses deep, abiding, unselfish friendship. Modern American society preaches *me first*. Paul's words urge us to serve voluntarily as understudies and second-stringers. Proverbs speaks of "a friend who sticks closer than a brother" (Proverbs 18:24). We should be that friend.

Paul told the Romans to be zealous and "keep your spiritual fervor" (Rom. 12:11). As a third-grader searching for a word beginning with the letter z for Mrs. Stigler's dictionary assignment, I discovered the word "zeal." Those four letters pack a punch: *passionate devotion, eager enthusiasm, fiery fervor.* That should describe our love for God and our love for other believers—zealous and with spiritual ardor, a flame that never flickers.

> *Engaging in ministry is evidence of the Spirit.*

As Christians, we demonstrate our joyful hope through service (12:11–12a). Engaging in ministry is evidence of the Spirit. See 12:13 also.

Patience isn't a twenty-first century virtue. Obviously it wasn't a first century virtue either. Paul wrote the Roman Christians to be "patient in affliction" and "faithful in prayer" (12:12).

Christian love in hard times looks like patience and faithful praying (12:12). In difficulty, we should pray fervently and constantly (see 1 Thessalonians 5:17). After Jesus ascended, that's what Jesus' followers did (Acts 1:13–14).

In Romans 12:13, Paul urged, "Share with God's people who are in need. Practice hospitality." Unfortunately, sharing doesn't come naturally—just watch toddlers. But love overcomes selfishness. Such sharing includes across the street and across the world. In Bible times when hotels and restaurants existed only as sparse inns, hospitality meant making beds and cooking meals. Missionaries serving in rural Africa offer that kind of hospitality today. But for most of us, offering hospitality means opening our homes for friendship, fellowship, and furthering God's kingdom.

After addressing love within the Christian community, Paul explained in Romans 12:14–21 how Christian love looks outside the church. Most of us don't understand persecution the way the Romans did or even the way believers in some countries do today, but we do know about personality conflicts, unkind words, and spiteful actions. As followers of Christ, we should "bless those who persecute" us and "not curse" them. Jesus said, "Love your enemies and pray for those who persecute you" (Matthew 5:44).

Paul knew that in times of great joy and great sorrow, Christians could have a significant impact on believers and non-believers. So we are to "rejoice with those who rejoice" and "mourn with those who mourn" (Rom. 12:15). In the course of a Saturday and Sunday while writing this lesson, I attended a funeral, two weddings, and a second funeral. That weekend, I soaked four handkerchiefs. Jesus himself "wept" with others (John 11:35).

Pride and conceit know no boundaries. Ego and vanity destroy unity in the church and hinder relationships with the lost, especially when we or church leaders aren't "willing to associate with people of low position" (Rom. 12:16). Arrogance and snobbery undermine Christian witness, whether in Paul's day or ours.

Paul stepped on lots of toes when he addressed how to treat enemies. "Do not repay anyone evil for evil" (12:17). Search the online bookstores and you will find that more than one author has written a book with the title *Don't Get Mad, Get Even* or some variation of those words. Revenge, like selfishness, seems inborn. When our son Marshall was three, he bit a two-year-old—something as far as we knew he had never done. John and I confronted him: "Biting isn't nice. It hurts. Don't bite again!"

. . . Love overcomes selfishness.

Marshall replied, "But he bit my baby brother." Sure enough, Michael sported teeth imprints. But genuine, sincere love has no room for revenge. Revenge never lives in love's house. Paul explained in Romans 12:19–21 how we must "overcome evil with good." Living "at peace with everyone" must be our goal (12:18).

Every Day, Everywhere, Live in Submission (13:1–7)

I grew up in the home of a "governing authority" (13:1). My father served as the county attorney in Eldorado, Texas, and my grandfather as justice

Baptists and the Bill of Rights

Settlers who came to the New World brought with them established state religion that mandated religious taxes and compulsory church attendance. Except in Pennsylvania and Rhode Island, Baptists faced imprisonment and flogging.

In 1777 Baptist minister John Leland moved to Virginia and led the fight for religious liberty. James Madison, having listened to Baptists preaching from jails, concluded the wrongness of state-established religion. In 1785, with support from Madison and Leland, Thomas Jefferson introduced the "Bill for Establishing Religious Freedom," effectively ending persecution of Baptists and Presbyterians in Virginia.

In 1787 when the Constitutional Convention sent the Constitution to the states, Leland led Virginia Baptists' opposition because the document didn't strictly guarantee religious liberty. Some thought the Baptist vote might defeat the ratification convention candidate James Madison and the constitution in Virginia. Leland and Madison met. The Baptist minister agreed to support Madison and the document if Madison promised to support an amendment guaranteeing religious freedom. True to his word, in 1789 Madison introduced the Bill of Rights, including the First Amendment concerning establishment of religion, which was ratified in 1791.[1]

of the peace. I spent hours typing legal documents in the county clerk's office and looked forward to coffee breaks with officials in the courthouse. I learned early the responsibility of government and my responsibility as a citizen.

Many wonder at Paul's insertion of instruction about government and citizenship in the midst of this passage. But Paul understood the necessity of living out faith in the world and the importance of order in spreading the gospel of love. Indeed, Roman roads and stability assisted in his missionary work.

Ego and vanity destroy unity in the church and hinder relationships with the lost. . . .

Earlier, the Roman Emperor Claudius had expelled Jews from Rome, including Aquila and Priscilla (Acts 18:1–3). On returning, Christians needed to be model subjects. Others believe Paul looked favorably on Rome because he enjoyed protection as a citizen. After all, his persecution came primarily from Jews. In fact, the Roman authorities later saved him from flogging and death in Jerusalem (Acts 22—23).

While Paul offered specific advice to the Roman church, his general message appears to include all Christians of all times. Paul understood that government exists under the authority of God (Rom. 13:1). Does that mean all governments are good? No. Does that mean God can and does use governing authorities for his purposes? Yes. Does that mean we should blindly follow wicked rulers because "rebelling against the authority is rebelling against what God has established" (13:2)? No. As "God's servant," the one in authority is subject to God's judgment (13:4; 1 Corinthians 4:1–5; 2 Corinthians 5:10).

Arrogance and snobbery undermine Christian witness, whether in Paul's day or ours.

However, if we prayerfully choose civil disobedience, we must prepare for consequences. Shadrach, Meshach, and Abednego refused to bow down to Nebuchadnezzar's golden statue and faced the fiery furnace (Daniel 3). Daniel disobeyed King Darius's edict to pray only to him. Daniel prayed to Yahweh and encountered lions (Dan. 6). In the twentieth century, some in South Africa cited Romans 13:1–7 to support government-mandated apartheid, and some in Nazi Germany used Paul's words to rationalize their non-opposition to Hitler. When our daughter Holly took a course in children's literature, I read her required list, including the 1990 Newbery Award winner *Number the Stars*. In that book, Lois Lowry weaves a fictional, real-life story about Jewish evacuation from Nazi-held Denmark. Narrated by ten-year-old Annemarie Johannesen, she tells how at great risk her family hid her best friend Ellen Rosen the evening before the Jewish round-up and smuggled the family to safety. Annemarie details how the women

When we love someone as we love ourselves, we want the best for the person.

cleaned their Jewish friends' homes during their absence. No, Paul doesn't write that government should *always* be obeyed. However, generally people "who do wrong" should fear authority and those who "do what is right" shouldn't (Rom.13:3).

Paul also called the Romans—and us—to "submit to the authorities . . . because of conscience" (13:5). Part of submitting to government means paying for it. My CPA husband gripes regularly about paying taxes although he earns income filing tax forms. Yet, we must all pay what we owe—taxes, bills, respect, and honor (13:6–7).

Hebrews 13:17 beautifully summarizes, "Obey your leaders and submit to their authority. They keep watch over you as men who must give an

Responsible United States Citizens

Consider these rights, responsibilities, and privileges of citizenship. Note those that enable citizens to take action when disagreeing with governmental laws or decisions:

- Nominating candidates to run for office
- Becoming informed about candidates and issues
- Voting for candidates and on referendums such as bond issues
- Holding public office
- Serving on juries
- Volunteering for councils or commissions
- Supporting political candidates with time and money
- Contacting public officials
- Attending forums, hearings, and open government meetings (school board, city council)
- Paying taxes

account. Obey them so that their work will be a joy, not a burden, for that would be of no advantage to you."

Every Day, Everywhere, Live in Love (13:8–10)

As a college student I taught preschoolers in their mission study time, Mission Friends. As the preschoolers played in art, blocks, and home living, we told them: *God loves you. God loves everyone. God wants you to love everyone. Some people don't know God loves them. We should tell them.*

Paul expressed that same concept by explaining our debt of love, "the continuing debt" we can never repay (13:8). Earlier in Romans, he extended this obligation "to Greeks and non-Greeks" (1:14). After enumerating some of the Old Testament commandments that are tied closely to relationships—adultery, murder, theft, and covetousness (13:9; see Exodus 20:13–15, 17), Paul boiled down the commandments to one rule, "Love your neighbor as yourself" (Rom. 13:9; Leviticus 19:18). When we love someone as we love ourselves, we want the best for the person. This applies every day, everywhere—within and beyond the Christian community.

Every Day, Everywhere, Live in Light (13:11–14)

Perhaps as a child, you sang, "This Little Light of Mine." I liked pointing my index finger and circling to the words, "I'm gonna let it shine." At first I didn't understand about hiding "it [Christ's light] under a bushel" until my teacher brought a bushel basket to church, covered the light, and showed us darkness.

. . . By maintaining lovingly positive relationships with other believers, governmental authorities, and all our neighbors, we glow with God's light in the world, drawing people to our Lord and Savior Jesus Christ.

Paul used the image of light, along with images of sleep and clothing, to call Christians to a moral lifestyle and bring us full circle to Romans 12:1–2. First, we wake up to what God is doing and will do (Rom. 13:11). Next, we turn on "the armor of light," turning off "deeds of darkness" and behaving "decently, as in the daytime" (13:12–13). Finally, like putting on clothing, we put on God's righteousness and take off "the desires of the sinful nature" (13:14).

When we, as Christians, live in sincerity, submission, and love every day and everywhere, we offer our "bodies as living sacrifices, holy and pleasing to God" without conforming "to the pattern of this world" but being "transformed by the renewing of your mind" (12:1–2). Too, by maintaining lovingly positive relationships with other believers, governmental authorities, and all our neighbors, we glow with God's light in the world, drawing people to our Lord and Savior Jesus Christ.

QUESTIONS

1. Recall a time you honored someone above yourself. Was it hard? Why or why not?

2. What are three specific ways we can offer hospitality to Christians and to non-Christians?

3. Why do pride and vanity cause disunity in the church?

4. Under what circumstances would you feel justified in disobeying a law or ordinance? Would you willingly accept the consequences? Why or why not?

5. How can we "put on the armor of light" and "put aside the deeds of darkness" (Rom. 13:12)?

NOTES

1. See Bill J. Leonard, *Baptist Ways: A History* (Valley Forge, Pennsylvania: Judson Press, 2003), 130–131.

Focal Text

Romans 14:1–21

Background

Romans 14:1—15:13

Main Idea

Christians should avoid condemning and judging one another but should seek harmony and offer mutual encouragement.

Question to Explore

What can we do to decrease if not erase the condemnation and judgment that lead to division among Christians?

Study Aim

To identify ways for ending the condemnation and judgment that lead to division among Christians

Study and Action Emphases

- Affirm the Bible as our authoritative guide for life and ministry
- Develop a growing, vibrant faith
- Value all people as created in the image of God
- Equip people for servant leadership

LESSON THIRTEEN Welcome Christians with Whom You Disagree

Quick Read

Paul called the Christians in Rome to neither condemn nor judge one another but to build one another up and live in the righteousness, peace, and joy of God.

137

Perhaps like me, you couldn't wait to get your driver's license. When I got my driver's license, our state deemed fourteen-year-olds mature enough to take the road after passing driver's education. Unfortunately, my school offered the course in June. I faced a difficult choice: forget summer camp or forget driving for a while. Finally, Mother devised a solution. My great-aunt counseled at camp and had driver's education certification. Would she instruct me? She agreed, and I spent every spare moment reading, discussing, re-reading, and re-discussing the driver's license handbook. My instructor believed in perfection. She demanded *100* on her practice tests. As a result, I dreamed in traffic-colors and knew the shape, wording, and meaning of every highway sign—from "cattle crossing" and "bridge out" to "stop" and "yield."

Obviously, the Apostle Paul never taught driver's education, but he knew how to post signs for Christians—in this case, for those in Rome. We'll use the idea of traffic signs to guide our study of this passage. Consider the "signs" Paul posted in this passage to the Roman Christians, who were having difficulty getting along with one another.

Romans 14:1–21

¹Accept him whose faith is weak, without passing judgment on disputable matters. ²One man's faith allows him to eat everything, but another man, whose faith is weak, eats only vegetables. ³The man who eats everything must not look down on him who does not, and the man who does not eat everything must not condemn the man who does, for God has accepted him. ⁴Who are you to judge someone else's servant? To his own master he stands or falls. And he will stand, for the Lord is able to make him stand.

⁵One man considers one day more sacred than another; another man considers every day alike. Each one should be fully convinced in his own mind. ⁶He who regards one day as special, does so to the Lord. He who eats meat, eats to the Lord, for he gives thanks to God; and he who abstains, does so to the Lord and gives thanks to God. ⁷For none of us lives to himself alone and none of us dies to himself alone. ⁸If we live, we live to the Lord; and if we die, we die to the Lord. So, whether we live or die, we belong to the Lord.

⁹For this very reason, Christ died and returned to life so that he might be the Lord of both the dead and the living. ¹⁰You, then, why do you judge your brother? Or why do you look down on your brother? For we will all stand before God's judgment seat. ¹¹It is written:

"'As surely as I live,' says the Lord,
'every knee will bow before me;
every tongue will confess to God.'"
[12] So then, each of us will give an account of himself to God.
[13] Therefore let us stop passing judgment on one another. Instead, make up your mind not to put any stumbling block or obstacle in your brother's way. [14] As one who is in the Lord Jesus, I am fully convinced that no food is unclean in itself. But if anyone regards something as unclean, then for him it is unclean. [15] If your brother is distressed because of what you eat, you are no longer acting in love. Do not by your eating destroy your brother for whom Christ died. [16] Do not allow what you consider good to be spoken of as evil. [17] For the kingdom of God is not a matter of eating and drinking, but of righteousness, peace and joy in the Holy Spirit, [18] because anyone who serves Christ in this way is pleasing to God and approved by men.
[19] Let us therefore make every effort to do what leads to peace and to mutual edification. [20] Do not destroy the work of God for the sake of food. All food is clean, but it is wrong for a man to eat anything that causes someone else to stumble. [21] It is better not to eat meat or drink wine or to do anything else that will cause your brother to fall.

Stop (14:1–6)

A stop sign contains no ambiguity. Stop now. Stop completely. My husband John learned the hard way late one night when he rolled through the red octagon. Paul's instructions leave no ambiguity. He well understood the importance of the Roman church. Not only did Rome occupy the honor as capital of the empire, but also the city would play a crucial role in spreading the gospel. A bickering, judgmental church or a condescending congregation could not rise to the challenge.

Although the Apostle had not yet visited the Roman Christians, he understood their division, division he believed needed to stop. In the rearview mirror of today, the conflicts may seem trivial—what to eat and when to observe special days. But then some of today's conflicts might well seem unimportant to the Romans, too. The issues in first-century Rome evidently didn't involve the essence of the gospel.

In Galatians, Paul made his position clear on matters essential to salvation, showing he never sought peace at any price (Galatians 1:6–7).

But he preached tolerance on inconsequential matters, matters that were inherently neither right nor wrong.

Paul realized that issues about inconsequential matters separated the church in Rome into two camps. He referred to one group as "weak" and the other as "strong," including himself among the "strong" (Romans 14:1; 15:1). The strong looked down on the weak, and the weak criticized the strong. Probably the strong numbered many Gentiles and a few mature Jewish Christians who believed salvation through Jesus negated the Old Testament food laws (Leviticus 11). Their faith offered freedom to move beyond the legalism that determined what to eat, how to prepare it, and with whom to eat it. The tradition-bound weak, on the other hand, continued religiously observing the old rules. Each group condemned the other.

> *. . . He preached tolerance on inconsequential matters, matters that were inherently neither right nor wrong.*

Lest we also condemn them, imagine following a family tradition for years and suddenly being told not to. When our children were small, we ate baked potatoes every Wednesday after church. One night when I dared fix something different, the complaints ranged from *Mother, how could you?* to *But we have baked potatoes every Wednesday* and *It's a family tradition*. The source of the conflict between the weak and the strong in Rome would have been even more intense because the source of the conflict went much deeper, being based on strongly-held religious and cultural beliefs.

First, Paul addressed the strong. He indicated they were critical and urged them to "accept him whose faith is weak, without passing judgment" (Rom. 14:1). He understood their Christian faith allowed them "to eat everything" but that the weak ate "only vegetables" (14:2). Although Jewish law didn't require a vegetarian diet, the Jews in the city probably had difficulty buying kosher meat and so avoided meat altogether. While this situation seems a bit different from eating meat sacrificed to idols in 1 Corinthians 8—10, Paul offered similar advice.

Paul stated that the Christian who "eats everything must not" disdain or scorn the Christian "who does not" (14:3). The mature in faith understood the implications of Jesus' sacrifice for the old laws, but they evidently were insensitive about relationships. Likewise, the one who doesn't "eat everything must not condemn the man who does" (14:3). Why should each group accept the other? Paul wrote that God accepted both. The

Apostle noted that only the master is authorized to judge his servants (14:4). In other words, only God can judge.

Then Paul moved to part two of the squabble. Again, the groups judged and condemned each other. The weak observed special days, perhaps Jewish festivals (note that Paul was more forceful about this in Gal. 4:10–11, likely because the situation was different in some way). Some Bible scholars believe the controversy also involved the primary day of worship—the traditional Sabbath or seventh day of the week versus the Lord's resurrection day or Sunday, the first day of the week (Acts 20:7). As Paul did with the matter of eating meat, he laid out the issue, noted that each Christian should follow his or her conscience, told the two groups to "back off," and reminded them their first allegiance was to God (Rom. 14:5–6).

Paul explained that regardless of which days Christ's followers observe or whether they eat meat or vegetables, they should glorify God (14:6).

B.H. Carroll: Pastor, Educator, and Theologian

Born in 1843 in Mississippi into the family of a Baptist minister, Benajah Harvey Carroll moved with his family to Texas. There he entered Baylor College in Independence, Texas, at age sixteen. Service on the Texas frontier during the Civil War interrupted his education, but he later received his bachelor's degree. B.H. Carroll accepted Christ after the war and quickly surrendered to preach. First Baptist, Waco, called him as pastor, where he served from 1870 to 1899. While in Waco, he taught at Baylor and helped organize its seminary in 1905. The seminary became Southwestern Baptist Theological Seminary in 1908. Carroll served as the founding president, a position he held until his death in 1914.[2]

Carroll's *Interpretation of the English Bible*[3] contains a list of the duties of individual Christians based on Romans 14, summarized as follows:

1. Don't split hairs. Accept each other.
2. Don't judge. That says look at me and not at God.
3. Don't put obstacles in others' paths.
4. Don't let bitterness create disagreement. Do what makes peace.
5. Don't be stubborn. In prayer, realistically assess your own faults to better bear those of others.
6. Don't sacrifice principle, but when possible, please others.

Whatever we do, we are to do so "to the Lord and give thanks to God" (14:6). The Message translation of the Bible says, "If you eat meat, eat it to the glory of God and thank God for prime rib; if you're a vegetarian, eat vegetables to the glory of God and thank God for broccoli" (14:6).[1]

Wrong Way (14:7–12)

Growing up in a small town, I had never seen a one-way street until our school superintendent drove us to the state capital for state literary competitions. Obviously, Mr. Humphries hadn't seen one either. Cars honked as he blissfully traveled the wrong way. The police flagged us down, patiently explained traffic flow, and let the superintendent off with a warning. My teen-age embarrassment made me want to hide in the floorboard, but we survived. Tragically, some drivers harm themselves and others by ignoring one-way signs.

Our conduct inspires others—positively or negatively.

Just as no one's driving affects himself or herself alone, so our lives consciously and unconsciously affect others. A wise friend explains the two major sources of power as being money and influence. When Paul wrote "none of us lives to himself alone," he showed he understood influence well (14:7). Influence permeates relationships and persists beyond death. Christians belong to the Lord forever (14:8–9). Therefore, Paul explained, lives should be lived "to the Lord" (14:6). Our conduct inspires others—positively or negatively.

. . . He laid out the issue, noted that each Christian should follow his or her conscience, told the two groups to "back off," and reminded them their first allegiance was to God (Rom. 14:5–6).

A pastor I know takes prospective staff to a busy restaurant marked by long waits in large crowds. Then the minister watches how the interviewee treats the hostess, handles the elbowing mob, reacts to the out-of-control children, and speaks to the harried wait staff. Occasionally, an otherwise suitable candidate fails the influence test.

If we as Christians don't always pass the influence test, Paul asked, ". . . Why do you judge your brother? Or why do you look down on your brother?" (14:10). To personalize his point, Paul changed from "we" in verse 8 to the singular "you" in verse 10. He then emphasized that every

What Would You Say?
What Would You Do?

1. You've invited for pizza a family newly-converted to Christianity from Islam. Your children want pepperoni, but you remember some missionaries told you that Muslims don't eat pork.
2. You're the pastor of a conservative church. The youth have asked to hold a dance in the fellowship hall as an outreach to their lost friends.
3. Bambi previously worked in the adult entertainment industry but recently became a Christian. Knowing about her beautiful voice, the worship leader invited her to perform a solo. However, she wore a somewhat revealing dress that showed her tattoos, and she sang in a manner more suitable to clubs than to church.

Christian will ultimately "stand before God's judgment seat" (14:10). Paul knew the Roman judgment seat well. On a mission trip, I saw where archaeologists had excavated the *bema* or judgment seat in Corinth. There, alone in the crowd, Paul had faced the powerful proconsul Gallio on charges of "persuading the people to worship God in ways contrary to the law" (Acts 18:13). In Romans, Paul quoted Isaiah 45:23, saying that at God's judgment seat, our knees will bow, our tongues will confess, and we will each "give an account . . . to God" (Rom. 14:11–12). Jesus said, "Do not judge, or you too will be judged. For in the same way you judge others, you will be judged, and with the measure you use, it will be measured to you" (Matthew 7:1–2).

> *We should willingly limit our freedom in inconsequential matters, giving the weak time and room to grow.*

Yield (14:13–21)

Paul shifted gears in Romans 14:13, from calling the Romans to stop passing judgment and going the wrong way to instructing them to avoid putting "any stumbling block or obstacle in your brother's way" (Rom. 14:13). The Apostle reasoned that an obstacle to one Christian may not be a stumbling block to another. Sometimes we need to yield even when we have the right-of-way.

In Mark 7:14–23, Jesus taught about the dietary laws. "Nothing outside a man can make him 'unclean' by going into him. Rather, it is what comes out of a man that makes him 'unclean'" (Mark 7:15). Although Jewish himself, Paul echoed his Savior, "As one who is in the Lord Jesus, I am fully convinced that no food is unclean in itself" (Rom. 14:14). However, the Apostle didn't stop with his own conscience. He continued with concern for others' consciences, writing, "But if anyone regards something as unclean, then for him it is unclean" (14:14).

Love trumps freedom.

Does that mean that even if the strong believed they had the freedom to eat non-kosher meat but another Christian sincerely didn't, the actions of the strong could be a stumbling block? Paul answered, *Yes.* If we knowingly distress others in nonessential matters, we fail to act in love (14:15). Winning arguments isn't important. We should willingly limit our freedom in inconsequential matters, giving the weak time and room to grow. True liberty is the liberty to deny self liberty. Love trumps freedom.

Paul continued that if we persist in judging other people for matters that really aren't very important, what we think is good can "be spoken of as evil" (14:16). After all, he said, God's kingdom doesn't consist of "eating and drinking, but of righteousness, peace and joy in the Holy Spirit" (14:17). In other words, be sensitive and please God (14:18). Give up and give in for "peace and . . . mutual edification" (14:19). Accept one another. Remember, we can't cross people off God's guest list or move their place cards. Too, doesn't dinner taste better at a peaceful table?

Perhaps you've heard of the "three-tell rule" for public speaking. (1) Tell them what you're going to tell them. (2) Tell them. (3) Tell them what you told them. Paul followed the rule. He wrote again not to destroy God's work "for the sake of food" (14:20). Instead, he said that it is better to voluntarily adjust what you eat and what you do rather than to "cause your brother to fall" (14:21). Family lore says a church removed my husband's grandfather from membership for playing the fiddle. What would Paul say? Using Christ as a yardstick, act cautiously. Follow your conscience but be sensitive, assuming others have reached their conclusions under God.

Caution (14:22—15:13)

A friend encouraged me to take her favorite countryside shortcut. As I rounded a sharp curve, I saw a yellow, caution, cattle crossing sign. I'm convinced Bossy read the sign, too. Just as I slowed, she looked at me, encouraged me to stop with a moo, and ambled across the lane, calf in tow.

Paul cautioned and encouraged in closing his letter's main body in 14:22—15:13. He explained that for a clear conscience, Christians must live by faith, basing their convictions on their relationship to God (14:22–23). The Apostle noted that Christ didn't please himself (15:1–3). Therefore, the "strong ought . . . not to please ourselves" but "should please his neighbor for his good, to build him up" (15:1–2). As Christians, we must forsake society's *me first* focus.

> As Christians, we must forsake society's me first *focus.*

In 15:4–13, Paul appealed for unity and acceptance of one another by quoting Scripture (2 Samuel 22:50; Psalm 18:49; Deuteronomy 32:43; Ps. 117:1; Isaiah 11:10). Then before concluding his letter with personal plans and greetings, Paul prayed the consequences of faith for the strong and the weak, "May the God of hope fill you with all joy and peace as you trust in him, so that you may overflow with hope by the power of the Holy Spirit" (Rom. 15:13).

Signs for a Purpose

Paul's letter offers guidance for church life today just as it did for the Romans. Sometimes we seem to find comfort in condemning and judging others. Too, we sometimes perceive others through the myopia of our own personal preferences. Or perhaps we unconcernedly glimpse fellow Christians through the blur of our own dirty windshields. Paul said we must see and act with the clarity Jesus gives.

Only then can we live Paul's beautiful benediction: "May the God who gives endurance and encouragement give you a spirit of unity among yourselves as you follow Christ Jesus, so that with one heart and mouth you may glorify the God and Father of our Lord Jesus Christ" (15:4–6). Don't we need that "spirit of unity . . . so that with one heart and mouth [we] may glorify the God and Father of our Lord Jesus Christ"? Only then can we spread the gospel "to the ends of the earth" (Acts 1:8).

QUESTIONS

1. What are some issues today that you believe could be classified as nonessential? What are some issues on which you could not give in?

2. What are some actions that need to be taken to avoid being a stumbling block to weaker Christians?

3. What do you think about this statement? *We burden the Christian message with legal, social, and cultural issues that are not the essence of the Christian faith.*

4. What are the differences between unity and uniformity?

5. How would you apply the adage, "Maximize what unites; minimize what divides," to Paul's teachings in this Scripture passage and to your own church?

6. When and how much should a Christian compromise to preserve unity in the church and denomination?

NOTES

1. Eugene H. Peterson, *The Message: the Bible in Contemporary Language* (Omaha, Nebraska: QuickVerse, 2002).
2. See "Benajah Harvey Carroll, " *Southern Baptist Historical Library and Archives Biographies*, www.sbhla.org/bio_bhcarroll.htm, accessed 11/9/2006. See also Harry Leon McBeth, *Texas Baptists: A Sesquicentennial History* (Dallas, Texas: BAPTISTWAY PRESS, 1998).
3. B. H. Carroll, *Interpretation of the English Bible*, vol. 12 (Nashville, Tennessee: Baptist Sunday School Board, 1916), 221–223.

THE GOSPEL OF MARK:
Jesus' Works and Words

UNIT ONE. GOOD NEWS TODAY

Lesson 1	Let Me Introduce Jesus	Mark 1:1–20
Lesson 2	A Faith Worth Acting On	Mark 2:1–12
Lesson 3	Live the Unbound Life	Mark 2:18—3:6

UNIT TWO. SHOWING WHO JESUS IS

Lesson 4	More Than Meets the Eye	Mark 4:21–34
Lesson 5	Jesus and Hopeless Situations	Mark 4:35—5:43
Lesson 6	When Cleanliness Is Not Next to Godliness	Mark 7:1–23
Lesson 7	There Are None So Blind	Mark 8:11–26

UNIT THREE. WITH JESUS ON THE WAY TO THE CROSS

Lesson 8	Not an Easy Way	Mark 8:27–38
Lesson 9	Me First	Mark 9:30–37
Lesson 10	Disciple = Servant	Mark 10:32–45
Lesson 11	Discipleship in Dangerous Times	Mark 13:1–13, 32–37
Lesson 12	Not Me	Mark 14:10–31
Lesson 13	The Worst and Best of Times	Mark 14:61b–64; 15:9–24, 37–41; 16:1–8
Christmas Lesson	Glory to God!	Luke 2:1–20

Additional Resources for Studying the Gospel of Mark:[1]

William Barclay. *The Gospel of Mark*. Revised edition. Philadelphia: The Westminster Press, 1975.

James A. Brooks. *Mark*. The New American Commentary. Volume 23. Nashville, Tennessee: Broadman Press, 1991.

Sharyn Dowd. *Reading Mark: A Literary and Theological Commentary on the Second Gospel*. Reading the New Testament Series. Macon, Georgia: Smyth and Helwys Publishing, 2000.

David E. Garland. *Mark*. The NIV Application Commentary. Grand Rapids, Michigan: Zondervan Publishing House, 1996.

Craig S. Keener. *IVP Bible Background Commentary: New Testament*. Downers Grove, Illinois: InterVarsity Press, 1993.

William L. Lane. *The Gospel According to Mark*. The New International Commentary on the New Testament. Grand Rapids, Michigan: William B. Eerdmans Publishing Company, 1974.

Lloyd J. Ogilvie. *Life Without Limits*: Waco, Texas: Word Books, Publisher, 1975.

Pheme Perkins. "Mark." *The New Interpreter's Bible*, Volume VIII. Nashville, Tennessee: Abingdon Press, 1995.

A. T. Robertson. *Word Pictures in the New Testament*. Volume I. Nashville, Tennessee: Broadman Press, 1930.

NOTES

1. Listing a book does not imply full agreement by the writers or BAPTISTWAY with all of its comments.

How to Order More Bible Study Materials

It's easy! Just fill in the following information. For additional Bible study materials, see www.baptistwaypress.org or get a complete order form of available materials by calling 1-866-249-1799 or e-mailing baptistway@bgct.org.

Title of item	Price	Quantity	Cost
This Issue:			
Romans: What God Is Up To—Study Guide (BWP001019)	$2.95	_____	_____
Romans: What God Is Up To—Large Print Study Guide (BWP001020)	$3.15	_____	_____
Romans: What God Is Up To—Teaching Guide (BWP001021)	$3.45	_____	_____
Additional Issues Available:			
Genesis 12—50: Family Matters—Study Guide (BWP000034)	$1.95	_____	_____
Genesis 12—50: Family Matters—Large Print Study Guide (BWP000032)	$1.95	_____	_____
Genesis 12—50: Family Matters—Teaching Guide (BWP000035)	$2.45	_____	_____
Leviticus, Numbers, Deuteronomy—Study Guide (BWP000053)	$2.35	_____	_____
Leviticus, Numbers, Deuteronomy—Large Print Study Guide (BWP000052)	$2.35	_____	_____
Leviticus, Numbers, Deuteronomy—Teaching Guide (BWP000054)	$2.95	_____	_____
Joshua, Judges—Study Guide (BWP000047)	$2.35	_____	_____
Joshua, Judges—Large Print Study Guide (BWP000046)	$2.35	_____	_____
Joshua, Judges—Teaching Guide (BWP000048)	$2.95	_____	_____
1 and 2 Samuel—Study Guide (BWP000002)	$2.35	_____	_____
1 and 2 Samuel—Large Print Study Guide (BWP000001)	$2.35	_____	_____
1 and 2 Samuel—Teaching Guide (BWP000003)	$2.95	_____	_____
Job, Ecclesiastes, Habakkuk, Lamentations: Dealing with Hard Times—Study Guide (BWP001016)	$2.75	_____	_____
Job, Ecclesiastes, Habakkuk, Lamentations: Dealing with Hard Times—Large Print Study Guide (BWP001017)	$2.85	_____	_____
Job, Ecclesiastes, Habakkuk, Lamentations: Dealing with Hard Times—Teaching Guide (BWP001018)	$3.25	_____	_____
Psalms and Proverbs: Songs and Sayings of Faith—Study Guide (BWP001000)	$2.75	_____	_____
Psalms and Proverbs: Songs and Sayings of Faith—Large Print Study Guide (BWP001001)	$2.85	_____	_____
Psalms and Proverbs: Songs and Sayings of Faith—Teaching Guide (BWP001002)	$3.25	_____	_____
Jesus in the Gospel of Mark—Study Guide (BWP000066)	$1.95	_____	_____
Jesus in the Gospel of Mark—Large Print Study Guide (BWP000065)	$1.95	_____	_____
Jesus in the Gospel of Mark—Teaching Guide (BWP000067)	$2.45	_____	_____
Luke: Journeying to the Cross—Study Guide (BWP000057)	$2.35	_____	_____
Luke: Journeying to the Cross—Large Print Study Guide (BWP000056)	$2.35	_____	_____
Luke: Journeying to the Cross—Teaching Guide (BWP000058)	$2.95	_____	_____
The Gospel of John: The Word Became Flesh—Study Guide (BWP001008)	$2.75	_____	_____
The Gospel of John: The Word Became Flesh—Large Print Study Guide (BWP001009)	$2.85	_____	_____
The Gospel of John: The Word Became Flesh—Teaching Guide (BWP001010)	$3.25	_____	_____
Acts: Toward Being a Missional Church—Study Guide (BWP001013)	$2.75	_____	_____
Acts: Toward Being a Missional Church—Large Print Study Guide (BWP001014)	$2.85	_____	_____
Acts: Toward Being a Missional Church—Teaching Guide (BWP001015)	$3.25	_____	_____

2 Corinthians: Taking Ministry Personally—Study Guide (BWP000008)	$2.35	_____	_____
2 Corinthians: Taking Ministry Personally—Large Print Study Guide (BWP000007)	$2.35	_____	_____
2 Corinthians: Taking Ministry Personally —Teaching Guide (BWP000009)	$2.95	_____	_____
1, 2 Timothy, Titus, Philemon—Study Guide (BWP000092)	$2.75	_____	_____
1, 2 Timothy, Titus, Philemon—Large Print Study Guide (BWP000091)	$2.85	_____	_____
1, 2 Timothy, Titus, Philemon—Teaching Guide (BWP000093)	$3.25	_____	_____
Hebrews and James—Study Guide (BWP000037)	$1.95	_____	_____
Hebrews and James—Teaching Guide (BWP000038)	$2.45	_____	_____
Revelation—Study Guide (BWP000084)	$2.35	_____	_____
Revelation—Large Print Study Guide (BWP000083)	$2.35	_____	_____
Revelation—Teaching Guide (BWP000085)	$2.95	_____	_____

Coming for use beginning December 2007

Mark:Jesus' Works and Words—Study Guide (BWP001022)	$2.95	_____	_____
Mark:Jesus' Works and Words—Large Print Study Guide (BWP001023)	$3.15	_____	_____
Mark:Jesus' Works and Words—Teaching Guide (BWP001024)	$3.45	_____	_____

Standard (UPS/Mail) Shipping Charges*	
Order Value	Shipping charge
$.01—$9.99	$5.00
$10.00—$19.99	$6.00
$20.00—$39.99	$7.00
$40.00—$79.99	$8.00
$80.00—$99.99	$11.00
$100.00—$129.99	$13.00
$130.00—$149.99	$17.00
$150.00—$199.99	$20.00
$200.00—$299.99	$25.00
$300.00 and up	10% of order value

Cost of items (Order value) _____
Processing fee (1% of Cost of Items) _____
Shipping charges (see chart*) _____
TOTAL _____

*Plus, applicable taxes for individuals and other taxable entities (not churches) within Texas will be added. Please call 1-866-249-1799 if the exact amount is needed prior to ordering.

Please allow three weeks for standard delivery. For express shipping service: Call 1-866-249-1799 for information on additional charges.

YOUR NAME _____ PHONE _____

YOUR CHURCH _____ DATE ORDERED _____

MAILING ADDRESS _____

CITY _____ STATE _____ ZIP CODE _____

MAIL this form with your check for the total amount to
BAPTISTWAY PRESS, Baptist General Convention of Texas,
333 North Washington, Dallas, TX 75246-1798
(Make checks to "Baptist Executive Board.")

OR, **FAX** your order anytime to: 214-828-5376, and we will bill you.

OR, **CALL** your order toll-free: 1-866-249-1799
(M-Th 8:30 a.m.-8:30 p.m.; Fri 8:30 a.m.-5:00 p.m.), and we will bill you.

OR, **E-MAIL** your order to our internet e-mail address:
baptistway@bgct.org, and we will bill you.

OR, **ORDER ONLINE** at www.baptistwaypress.org.

We look forward to receiving your order! Thank you!